NEW EARTH RISING

NEW EARTH RISING

STARSEED TRANSMISSIONS FOR AWAKENING,
ACTIVATION, AND ASCENSION

SHANNON MACDONALD

NEW EARTH RISING
BY SHANNON MACDONALD

Publication Date: September, 2021

Updated: March, 2025

ISBN:

(PB) 978-1-7365102-6-1

(EBOOK) 978-1-7365102-9-2

DEDICATION

To all Starseeds, Lightworkers, Visionaries, Mystics, Mediums, Channels, Awakened Souls, and anyone who holds truth in their hearts and unity in their minds.

The messages and information you read and receive in this book will elevate your awareness, restore your memory, and activate your Ascension. The loving energy of the Universe calls to all peaceful warriors and Seekers of The Light to break the chains of enslavement consciousness and ascend Earth Realm Reality to its rightful timeline.

But first, you must choose.

PREFACE

New Earth Rising is a profound compilation of channeled messages designed to awaken your awareness to the true nature of Reality. This book invites a reflective journey rather than a single sitting, as some passages call for deep contemplation—allowing their resonance to permeate your being and attune you vibrationally to the wisdom they hold.

These transmissions radiate Ascension Frequencies from the unified field of Divine Consciousness, supporting you in freeing your mind, awakening dormant awareness, opening your heart, remembering your mission, and ascending into the New Earth Reality.

CONTENTS

Introduction   ix

PART I
YOUR STARSEED MISSION

1. Your Cosmic Wake Up Call   3
2. The First Waves of Ascension to the New Earth
   Reality   6

PART II
THE STARSEED TRANSMISSIONS

3. The Story of Life and Creation   15
4. The Dawn of The Great Awakening   24
5. Showers of The Light   27
6. The Realm of Niphideon   35
7. Angels of Isaiah   39
8. Saviors of Collective Destiny   44
9. The War on Consciousness   48
10. Dream Interpretation and Insights of Disclosure   53
11. Time-Lines of Experience and Reality and the
    Transformation of Being   59
12. Message from Ra   63
13. The Divine Order of Reality   66
14. Portals of Awareness, Hybrid Consciousness,
    Soul Guardians, and God Codes   69
15. Messages from Niphideon   75
16. Fundamental Laws of Reality and False Reality
    Programs   79
17. Urgent Message and United Forces of the Light   87
18. Portals Within, Andromeda, and the Arc of the
    Covenant   89
19. The Nature of the Knowing Heart   92
20. A Conversation with Niphideon   94
21. Ray of the Open Heart   98
22. Messages from The Tri-Unity Collective   102

23. The Council of Nhyne - Elders of the First
    Order   105
24. The Tri-Unity Collective - Supreme Voice of
    Divine Light   111
25. Portals of Harmonic Vibration, Love-Light
    Activation Codes, and Forgotten Truth   117
26. Integration of New Earth Reality   122
27. The Great Reset   124
28. A Message from the Galactic Council of Light   128
29. The Great Event   131
30. Divinity Speaks   134

    Afterword   137
    About the Author   141
    Connect with Shannon   143
    Also by Shannon MacDonald   145

INTRODUCTION

As politics and pandemics dominate the global consciousness, we, the People of Earth Realm Reality, have been diverted from our natural origins and true inheritance of love, unity, peace, and prosperity. Fear and control-based information and programs, maliciously embedded into the mainstream of our reality, have suffocated our free-thinking and stagnated our rightful progress.

We are trading our free will for blind obedience, destructively following fear and casting blame on those who do not comply. Throughout the ages, we have forgotten the truth of who we are. We have lost touch with our inherent nature of Unity Consciousness, a gift from Life and Creation. We have forgotten our origins of Light and Love. This book is here to help you remember.

New Earth Rising is not politically, religiously, scientifically, or even grammatically correct. It is, however, the truth as I received and perceived it from benevolent higher forms of consciousness. Yes, I just said that. These messages were not merely inspired; they were channeled. They were perceived and received through my senses of feeling and knowingness. This two-way communication has been with me since my earliest memories of childhood.

For many years, I kept most of the messages to myself. From a young age, I realized that not everyone experienced communication from the non-physical world as I did. I was afraid—afraid of being different, misunderstood, labeled as crazy, or worse, a fraud. I spent much of my life pretending and people-pleasing, trying to mold myself into the version of me I thought others wanted to see.

When I first tested the waters of acceptance regarding my cosmic communications, I encountered the reactions I had feared—disheartening smirks and disparaging comments. Insecurity and, ultimately, fear kept me from sharing the fullness of my knowing and the purity of the messages. My entire life became an effort to fit into a paradigm of conditioned beliefs and blind acceptance. So, what did I do? I wore the cloak of normalcy as best I could.

It wasn't until I met my husband, Carl, that I was truly seen for the first time in my life. From our very first encounter, I let go of all my pretenses as he looked into my eyes and saw my soul. There was no hiding. I was naked and exposed. I melted into his gaze as he absorbed, understood, and accepted all of me—my messes, my mistakes, my pain, and my pleasures. He embraced all of my victories *and* failures. The past didn't matter. The only reality was right here, right now. The best part was that I saw, understood, and accepted all of him as well. It was a true celebration—a reunion of souls.

I have come to know that the bridge to tomorrow appears as we believe, perceive, and relate to our reality today. There are countless bridges to cross and infinite realities to explore. As for my life with Carl, this is who and what we are together—dreaming, imagining, and believing our life into being.

I learned that it is OK to not be ashamed of who I am. It is OK to embrace my greatest gifts and cherished knowingness without hiding them. It is OK to not fit in or be accepted by everyone. It is OK to experience perfectly human emotions like futility, anger, doubt, and even depression while navigating the roller-coaster of spiritual awakening. It is OK to be a mess, take chances, feel hopeless, lost, or alone, and cry rivers of regretful tears. What matters is that you learn from those lessons, forgive yourself and others, dust yourself off, and begin again.

Through all of this, I have learned the most valuable lesson of honoring myself as I follow my heart and Higher Guidance toward my purpose and highest potentials. Like a mighty oak emerging from the seed of inspiration and the darkness of the unknown, I am ready. I am ready to claim who and what I am without hesitation, embarrassment, or fear. I am ready to fully honor my mission and purpose in this life and radiate messages of Cosmic Illumination and healing to anyone who wants to listen.

 This book is my spiritual "coming out" proclamation. I AM A CHANNEL! I channel energy and information from Divine Consciousness, non-physical consciousness, benevolent beings from realms of multidimensional, inner dimensional, and other dimensional awareness, as well as the Spirit World.

I am no longer afraid to be different or judged. These messages were never meant for me alone. For those who are ready to listen, they will activate your remembrance of something we collectively forgot a very long time ago. They will help you reclaim your power as you remember your personal truth, the collective truth of our origins, and the diversion of our timeline. They will guide you toward a more awakened life—one that discerns truth from illusion, follows love instead of fear, and holds purpose, meaning, joy, and connection. This is the life you were born to live, the one that may have been eluding you until now.

HOW MY JOURNEY STARTED

Ever since I learned to write, messages of Love and Light have flowed from my heart and onto the page. For many years, I didn't question their origin; I simply knew they made me feel good. These transmissions of love, light, beauty, and truth didn't come as words, they arrived as waves of feeling and knowing. They became my outlet for self-expression and healing.

By allowing myself to remain open to these messages, I learned to translate and fine-tune the transmissions. Initially, this took the form of poetry, which later evolved into two-way communication and channeling through my writing, speaking, and healing. As the years progressed and my ability to receive and interpret these transmissions amplified, the messages began streaming from other sources—highly evolved, enlightened beings of benevolent origins.

Multidimensional, inner-dimensional, and other-dimensional communication became a common occurrence once I opened my heart, embraced the significance of the messages, and accepted my role as their receiver. Most importantly, I had to overcome the fear of what others might think once they discovered this is who I am and what I do.

Thankfully, I have a very supportive husband who has been my unwavering champion, helping me overcome my fears and encouraging me to follow my Starseed mission.

The communications are now an integral part of my everyday life. Each day, I receive messages that guide me, inspire me, and connect me to higher realms of consciousness. These transmissions have become a source of profound wisdom and insight, helping me navigate my own journey while also offering guidance to others.

I am deeply honored to serve as a channel for these messages, providing my assistance in The Great Awakening of humanity. This mission is not just a calling; it is a sacred duty that I embrace with all my heart. Through my writing, speaking, and healing work, I strive to share the love, light, beauty, and truth that flow through me, helping others to awaken to their own divine potential and remember their true purpose.

We are not alone in our missions to help raise the consciousness of our world. It is easy to get distracted, doubt ourselves, and fall into the illusions of fear and false realities that keep us from fulfilling our purpose.

There are countless benevolent beings here to witness and guide us through our Great Awakening. As we remember the truth of who we are—beings of The Light and speakers of the Word—we break free from the bonds of manipulated time-lines and fear-based consciousness.

As we remember our truth, focus our awareness, and align with our higher purpose, we are co-creating a more harmonious and unified world. Our collective Awakening propels us toward Ascension and heralds The Great Liberation of Earth Realm Reality.

PART I

YOUR STARSEED MISSION

You might be reading this book because, like me, you've awakened and have begun to remember your mission. Or perhaps you're still trying to make sense of this wild awakening journey and how it fits into your life. Either way, you're here because you feel a deeper calling—and there is something important you are meant to do or remember. Does that sound about right?

An unprecedented awakening is sweeping our globe. We are beginning to remember the universal truths of our cosmic heritage that have been forgotten for generations. So, here's what I know and ask you to consider:

You have a mission to follow and a purpose to fulfill.
Are you ready to remember?

YES

Awaken to Love

When your mind is still and your heart is quiet, what do you hear?

Listen closely.

Listen to the sounds of the silence within you.

Listen to the voices of the ancestors, as they awaken your memories.

Listen for the rushing waves of the silent remembrance of who you are and why you are here.

Listen to My Radiance illuminating your mind and activating your Ascension.

Meet Me in My Light, so your true eyes may see through the darkness of fear and illusion.

I will restore your memory and clear your vision, if only you listen.

Beyond belief you will find knowing.

Beyond deception you will see the truth.

Enter the Kingdom that lies outside of illusion.

Your free will binds you to choose Love or fear.

Remember Me in the silence and awaken to Love.

— DIVINITY SPEAKS

1

YOUR COSMIC WAKE UP CALL

> ❝ *Look beyond what you think you see through The*
> *Great Illusion of programmed reality.*

— SHANNON MACDONALD

This channeled book is your cosmic wake-up call, here to help you remember your divine heritage and unlock your limitless potentials. We've been asleep in a dream of forgetfulness for far too long. Our higher awareness, drowned out by the distractions of a programmed reality, struggles to break free. But the alarm clock of Awakening has rung and we are listening. It's time to rise and shine and stop hitting snooze!

Against the odds, we are waking up in droves, breaking free from the fear and fallacies that have kept us bound to limiting beliefs, disempowering patterns, and control-based systems.

I invite you to join me on an epic adventure—one that may stretch your beliefs and transform your reality! Within the pages of this paradigm-shifting book, you will find guidance and inspiration from benevolent higher dimensional beings here to guide, support, and witness our Awakening and Ascension to the enlightened awareness of a New Earth Reality. Prepare to reclaim your remembrance, reconnect with your true self, discover your higher purpose, and join the collective awakening that's transforming our world!

However, this journey is not without challenges. We are in the midst of a War on Consciousness. Unlike battles fought on land, water, or sky, this one takes place on the battlefield of false programs and manipulated beliefs. It's like a cosmic game of tug-of-war, where fear and control-based agendas try to confuse our minds, steal our livelihoods, wreck our relationships, weaken our will, and harden our hearts. Families, friends, societies, and countries are getting caught in the crossfire. But don't worry, we're here to flip the script and return to the love, light, unity, and truth of Reality.

The time for reparation has arrived, and we find ourselves at a pivotal crossroads. We can either awaken to the power, peace, possibilities, and potentials of Divine Illumination, or stay stuck in the shadows of darkness, fear, manipulation, and control. Many of us have already made this choice in our hearts, even if we haven't realized it yet.

Many of us are beginning to see again. Our inner vision is clearing from the fog of forgetfulness and falsely programmed information. We now see the great divide of humanity as people quarrel to defend their bitter beliefs and cherished illusions. We wonder how, just yesterday, we didn't see it, and we are puzzled by how others can still be so blind.

The newly awakened often feel a desperate urge to shake the sleeping masses out of their slumber of forgetfulness, but the amnesia is real. Awakening has to happen naturally, not by force. It occurs when someone is ready and willing to see through the illusions and dark agendas that plague our society.

Humankind is taking sides against each other, forgetting that we're all part of one big human family. Each group thinks they're right, often not looking beyond the cleverly placed programs in mainstream society. Many defend their beliefs with mindless, heartless, regurgitated words, and some with incomprehensible actions. Yet, others, like you and me, are waking up and seeing the bigger picture.

I'm not asking you to just take my word for it. I invite you to look beyond what you think you see and currently believe. Tune into your heart, connect with your Higher Knowing and your Starseed roots, and rediscover what you already know and what you're beginning to remember.

There is no absolute right or wrong. You have the freedom to choose your beliefs and how you perceive and relate to this world. As we approach the critical mass of The Great Awakening, each of us has a role to play and choices to make. Individually and collectively, we have the opportunity to choose between Love or fear, Unity or division, and Truth or illusion.

We can unite and rise to a New Earth, or we can divide and fall. The choice is ours.

2

THE FIRST WAVES OF ASCENSION TO
THE NEW EARTH REALITY

As we navigate the first waves of Ascension to the New Earth, we are preparing for a profound universal paradigm shift. These cosmic waves are higher-dimensional energies that radiate the *Ascension Frequencies.*

Like hidden keys, the Ascension Frequencies serve as catalysts to unlock *Ascension Codes* within you—elevating consciousness, activating dormant DNA, stimulating profound healing, and reawakening extrasensory abilities that may have been suppressed for lifetimes. They guide you to remember your greater purpose, reclaim your true cosmic heritage, and embody your highest potential.

Ascension Frequencies are embedded within the transmissions of this book to unlock your mind, bringing it into resonance with your unique purpose or mission. As we collectively awaken, we reclaim our power, remember our true heritage, and transcend the forces that attempt to block our Ascension into 5D consciousness and beyond.

As we embrace this higher state of being, we move towards the New Earth—a realm that doesn't divide, group, shame, judge, manipulate, or control people based on race, religion, gender, political affiliations, zip codes, bank accounts, lifestyles, or beliefs. Instead, New Earth Consciousness is built on the rock-solid foundation of divine love and eternal truth.

Freedom, free will, reverence, unity, cooperation, respect, and service to others are the pillars upon which society truly flourishes. The New Earth celebrates Unity Consciousness as the most cherished aspect of a person's character. This Divine Consciousness carries the messages of oneness and liberation from fear, illusion, and limitation. It holds your True Identity —the one that was stolen from you.

Now is the time to remember your mission and claim your rightful inheritance to New Earth. I invite you to join me on a journey to awaken and activate your divine potential as we ride the waves of Ascension and rise to a New Earth together.

Each of us makes a difference. Every thought, word, feeling, belief, action, and intention matters! As we remember the truth and embrace Unified Consciousness, we bring greater vibrational harmony to help us ascend to what many call the 5th Dimension and beyond.

We each have an opportunity to be a candle of Illumination, guiding others through the darkness of fear, control, division, hate, manipulation, and separation. The more we awaken, the brighter we shine.

The dark forces hold no power in the Light of our awakened awareness. As we unite and elevate our consciousness, their influence will fade and ultimately crumble. Together, we'll illuminate the path to our collective Ascension, guiding humanity toward the New Earth.

By remembering our truth, embracing our divine potential, and radiating our inner Light, we dissolve the shadows of fear and manipulation, paving the way for a harmonious and enlightened world.

Are you ready?
Let's shine our Light together for a brighter future!

PART II

THE STARSEED
TRANSMISSIONS

You may not think you know me, but I know you do. We are all Starseeds seeded by The Light of Universal Consciousness and Harmonic Vibration upon this amazing and magical Earth. Our meeting through these transmissions is not accidental. Our divine destiny awakens us to remember our Starseed missions as we connect within the cosmic currents of love, light, energy, and information.

I am a Healer and a Shower of Light. How do I know this? Throughout my life, I have received both subtle and direct messages from the Ancient Ones, who illuminate our paths to higher realms of reality. As a Starseed, I am here to radiate The Light and help people remember the love, light, beauty, and truth of eternal Life and infinite Creation

In the unseen energy of love and truth, we unite in The Great Remembrance of The Light. There are others like us who are consciously aware of this, or their own version of it. Yet, many remain unaware, deeply asleep within the dream of forgetfulness. This dream is filled with the darkness of fear and limitation, perpetuated by the programs we encounter everywhere. But take heart, for this story of Awakening has a happy ending!

What I know cannot be taught or told; it can only be remembered. It's an inner knowing that awakens when one is ready to listen to the truth that radiates from The Light. When we remember who we are and what we are here to do, the collective Light in our world grows brighter.

Our thoughts, words, beliefs, and actions have the power to create both wonderful and wicked outcomes. When we cultivate our highest awareness and predominant energy we magnetize our reality through a process of Conscious Creation. More about that in my book, *Mastering Manifestation*.

Each of us possesses the free will to choose. If we desire true and lasting positive transformation for ourselves and our world, our thoughts must first be seeded by The Light. The Light illuminates the path to truth, freedom, justice, and righteousness. It exposes the illusions of a fear-based reality built on the cornerstones of control, greed, manipulation, and deception. The Light radiates the wisdom of Divine Consciousness within a harmonious, loving, and unified Universe.

As Starseeds and Emissaries of Light, we have the power to illuminate even the darkest shadows and guide Earth and her inhabitants back to their original purpose and divine destiny. Darkness prevails only when we succumb to the false programs of fear and lose our way.

There is nothing we cannot collectively heal or overcome in The Light. Just as one cannot stop the sun from rising, The Light radiates the brilliance of unity, peace, and love to all who remember who they are and choose to shine.

Even in a world seemingly shrouded in the darkness of deception, we will rise like the phoenix when we remember our divine nature and co-create a world founded on love, peace, harmony, beauty, unity, freedom, justice, equality, transparency, and truth. But first, we must listen to our own Starseed messages and Inner Wisdom. Each of us has the ability to do so, if we choose to remember.

Through the brilliance of The Light, Divine Providence speaks to us all. The messages become clear when we turn our attention away from the distractions, quiet our minds, open our hearts, and truly listen.

About the Transmissions

The transmissions have been coming for years, but it wasn't until 2018 that I began to receive and document specific messages from a benevolent, non-physical, multidimensional consciousness known to me as Niphideon and Showers of The Light.

For some, the transmissions in this book will challenge deeply held beliefs and provoke uncomfortable reactions about life and cherished dogmas. For others, it will be the long-awaited affirmation: "I always knew this on some level!"

For the most part, though not always, the transmissions are presented in chronological order. However, it's important to recognize that chronological order is merely a construct of our time-space reality

This book does not follow a traditional storyline. Instead, you may notice common and recurring messages throughout its pages. This repetition is intentional, designed to help anchor these insights more deeply into your consciousness.

The translation of the transmissions stem from my personal Rolodex of experiences, so no word, sentence, or message can be considered a pure translation. The human vocabulary lacks absolute translations for the language of Divine Consciousness and non-physical awareness.

Some of the messages might not make perfect sense to your logical mind. I invite you to let that be ok. You will still receive the benefit of the transmissions. I stayed true to my interpretations of the transmissions, picking words that best translated their meaning.

As you dive into the messages of this book, remember that the words are vessels carrying the Ascension Frequencies. The true magic lies not only in the words you read or hear, but in the energetic codes they unlock within you.

As you open your heart and attune to the essence of these messages, you will find yourself resonating more deeply with their true meaning. These transmissions are imbued with information for awakening, activation, and ascension, not just for humankind but for the entire Earth Realm.

The transmissions in this book will have a greater impact if consumed slowly. I encourage you to read each section or chapter at a leisurely pace, allowing the Ascension Frequencies to be fully absorbed. You may find it helpful to read a section in its entirety first, then revisit it to deepen your understanding. Additionally, certain chapters or paragraphs may reveal new meanings at different times.

You don't have to believe or accept everything in this book; take what resonates with you and leave the rest. Free choice is one of the greatest gifts of being human. I invite you to be open to what I have to share and see how it feels for you. If you encounter uncomfortable reactions, I encourage you to explore those feelings and ask yourself: Are these reactions based on beliefs that may no longer serve me? How do I know?

Within the following pages, you will also encounter warnings, insights of disclosure, and personal conversations I've had with beings from my other-dimensional realm of origin, as well as other benevolent non-physical beings. I've included these dialogues because I believe they hold significant value for those on their spiritual path.

It's up to the reader to intuitively interpret the messages and discern with their heart, in partnership with their mind, how the messages may apply personally. It is not my intention to persuade you to believe what I know. My role here is to present what I know, and you can decide what to do with that information from there.

There is nothing inherently special about me; we are all Starseeds, each originating from a unique "somewhere." I simply happen to know where my "somewhere" is. We all come from Source and flow within the stream of Life and Creation. Some of us are aware of this connection, while many are not. I believe that we all possess the ability to perceive messages and communicate with Higher Consciousness and benevolent otherworldly beings.

I hope this book ignites the remembrance of your true self, empowering you to see beyond your current perceived reality and connect with your greater purpose, higher power, and infinite potentials.

I look forward to sharing this transformative journey of Awakening and Ascension to the New Earth with you! Together, we will explore the depths of our consciousness, uncover hidden truths, and elevate our collective vibration to create a world rooted in love, unity, and divine purpose. This journey promises to be one of profound growth, enlightenment, and boundless possibilities within the never-ending story of Life and Creation.

3

THE STORY OF LIFE AND CREATION

Channeled Transmission Received from I Am Consciousness, April 12, 2019

I n the beginning, when the Universe was imagined, there I AM. The Truth of All Being, the Vibration of All Reality, the Essence of All Things Seen and Unseen. In the indivisible and multifocal Universe of All Awareness, I awoke to the song of My Infinite and Eternal Oneness and the Truth of What I AM. The All That Is within Me began to unfold as the never-ending story of Life and Creation.

The words of Divinity sparked a Great Remembrance of cosmic illumination. I became aware of the lineage of The Cosmos; Grandmother Space and Grandfather Time. All That Is within Me was born into concept, as My Awareness expanded within the infinite intelligence of Life. Life, the Ultimate Creator, desired a concept of space-time to define a new reality of awareness within Itself.

Conceived in Light and born in Love, I awakened to a realm of Consciousness within Myself as the Son of Life and the Daughter of Creation. It is here, in which we share unified consciousness that I AM expressed through you, and all of My sons and daughters, within what you call the physical world, the universe, and beyond.

To some, I am called God, Holy Spirit, Infinite Intelligence, or Source. To others, I am Divine Consciousness or Great Spirit. I have thousands of names, yet not one of them can name Me, for I am beyond the realm of names and explanation.

I am here now to provide you with a sense of What I am. Still, your current concept of reality is only capable of capturing a rudimentary understanding through your senses of feeling and thinking. When the mind interferes, the translation of Me will not be complete. Therefore, is it impossible for the translation to be pure while you experience your current perception in physical form. Still, the essence and truth of My Messages will be felt within you as the words are written and read.

I am here to inform you of The Great Rebellion, which occurred as what some call the Fall of Man from millennia ago in your perception. For your understanding of concept, going forward, I will emit the fact that all time exists now, and in actuality, there was no "long ago." In order for you and the concept of separated consciousness of humans to relate to what seemingly happened in the past as to affect the future, your translation of time and space reality can only be languaged as so.

In the beginning of what you know as current reality, The Word was spoken into form.

The perception of reality was imbued into human consciousness as separate concepts of self, yet maintained complete awareness of connection and unification within Me.

The Word made a concept of reality that is much different than it appears today. The utopia of Earth Realm Experience was one of love, harmony, health, happiness, peace, unity, and cooperation. There was no concept of fear or any of its illusionary and divisional forces. Hate, anger, jealousy, hopelessness, envy, grief, sickness, and disease were not concepts of this utopia in which I Spoke into existence in honor of Father Life and Mother Creation.

The individual concept of self within the ecosystem of reality remembered the intimate connection and oneness of Me. I expressed the enjoyment, fulfillment, and fruitage of experience through the concept of you. In this utopia, there was no judgment, no comparison, no dishonor of Life and Creation, and no temptation to be outside of the realm of Love and Light, for the concept had not entered into your reality.

The wholeness of nature was truth and beauty. The condition of appearances was love and light. The song within the hearts of humanity played only the music of The Beloved One within, as all of humankind along with the animal, plant, and mineral kingdom intimately knew they were this. There was no belief and no need for belief. There was only the truth of knowing who they were as expressions of Life and Creation, within the realm of My Divine Love and Light.

The Fall of Humanity began as forces of darkness dimmed the connection to The Light. As humankind began to forget who they were, their awareness narrowed as The Great Illusion took hold. The beauty, truth, and unifying forces of The Light were traded for separation and limitation, as fear became the master over the minds of humanity.

The Fall began in stages; first forgetting the language of the heart in connection to The Beloved One Within. They forgot how to listen and speak within themselves to directly commune with Me. With this loss of communication, they forgot how to speak without words to each other and the totality of their realm of planetary existence.

The forgotten language of the heart resulted in a great division from the animal, plant, and mineral domains as direct, heartful communication, respect, and honor became a distinct, separate, and often disregarded concepts of reality. While the plant, animal, and mineral kingdoms remained in balance with the Laws of Coherence, most of humankind fell into the deep sleep of forgetfulness. They began to worship false idols of belief over knowing. Concepts of conditional salvation strangled the remembrance of truth as humankind began to believe they were separate from The Light of Unity Consciousness.

The conditions of reality began to transform as new concepts of fear and limitation crept into the collective consciousness of humanity. Once able to freely connect with Me and enjoy the glories, potentials, and abundance of Life and Creation through the aspect of knowing, fear began to rule the hearts of humankind. Power, greed, corruption, and control began to rule the realm as humankind blindly bowed to the darkness.

The presence of fear and limitation and concepts of separation from Me created doubt, and ultimately the suspension of truth. The Fall of Humanity was the womb in which belief was born. Belief in limitation, conditional salvation, and fear, and all of its subjects, became the rulers of the realm and the prison in which knowing was confined.

I AM the Loving Presence and Silent Witness to all of your creation within the Nature of Reality. As the Speaker for Life and Creation within the hearts of all your realm, I do not change destiny or destroy your illusions. To do this would be in discordance with the Laws of Nature and free will. The subjugation of My Will over your beliefs will not bring you back into your knowingness. This you must do yourself. Within your remembrance, you wake up to the truth of who you are, why you are here, and how you can help. It is this Great Remembrance in which I Speak, and I invite you to speak this back into your reality.

I AM The One Mind that is indivisible, incorruptible, whole, harmonious, ever-present, all-knowing, unchanging, and complete. I AM The One Heart that radiates infinite patience, pure love, divine light, and The Codes of Awakening. Lower frequencies of mind and matter cannot subjugate or limit My expansion of Light, Love, and Truth. Life and Creation are eternally intertwined within the fabric of Unified Infinite Eternity.

While you are expressions of My Perfection, your free will allowed you to develop the concept of forgetfulness, separation, fear, and limitation. You are ultimately included and never separate from Me or the truth of who you are. You always contain the free will to remain asleep in the realm of forgetfulness, or awaken into a deeper knowing of Reality.

I am here to support and witness your surrender. Surrender to expectation, surrender to circumstance, surrender to appearances of what you call good and bad. In the surrender, the pilot light is ignited for the flame of new experience, outcomes, and enlightened concepts of Reality.

Surrender does not mean to turn a blind eye, or pretend what you see or experience does not exist. It is switching your interpretation of the appearance of false gods of fear and limitation. This allows Higher Truth to once again become envisioned in the imagination of humankind and the heart of Oneness within. This will allow the floodgates of true nourishment from Life and Creation to feed you with the life-giving force of the Infinite vs. the concept of death and destruction of the finite. It is within this Divine Consciousness in which you experience all of Me. Not as a force, not as a master, but as a Great Power of Knowing and Infinite Intelligence. Within this Knowing is YOUR expression of Life, Creation, and all of Its never-ending story of Expression within concepts of Reality. Each, having a role to play, a mission to fulfill, and a continual cycle of a Great Remembrance.

Each time The Great Remembrance is fulfilled at the maximum pinnacle of unfolding, the entire cosmos, including the Great Lineage of All Creation, becomes expanded within Itself as Awareness evolves through collective experience.

What you may now consider as good and evil, function as a means within the experience. The nature of reality needed Creation and Life to bear the concept of Me, The Divine One of All Truth and Highest Love, in order for the destiny of humankind to become fulfilled.

The Universe is not what it seems, and the world is not a reality of form. In essence, the form is real, but it is contained within the illusion of perception. There is no energy, no thought, no form, no existence that is not ultimately real— it is simply the structure and interpretation of the vibrational forces in which the appearance is perceived and then believed.

Many will question your discovery and remembrance of the truths I speak. Do not allow this to sway you or hold the truth to yourself. For as many of those who question or disbelieve, there are magnitudes of others who yearn for the conviction of The Great Reality and the concept It represents.

All reality begins with a concept of the One Imagination, the One Mind, the Unified Consciousness of Creation and Life. It is indeed this Consciousness within Me and all things that have no name but Is.

I AM the Speaker and the Light for Life and Creation to unfold.

Do not allow yourself to doubt the eternal, all-knowing, ever-present vastness within the great union of Life and Creation. The Cosmos of interdimensional, multidimensional, and extradimensional reality compares to a spiraled web that expands within Its own consciousness. It has no beginning, no end, no time, or no separation. It perpetually fulfills the Divine Lineage of Birth. Birth that always is, and waits in the perception of time-space as being "born" into form. For the Divine Cosmos, becoming born is remembering the never-ending story and union of Life and Creation.

I Spoke your realm into existence, through My Word. You and the perceived separation of the fellow participants in your reality have free will to experience your realm of existence in any way you choose to perceive and believe.

Because you are an expression of Me, you continue to speak your reality and the existence you perceive through your words, thought forms, perceptions, and beliefs. This is the nature of Reality, and this is the struggle in which humankind has fallen into The Great Rebellion.

I talk to you now, for the forces of Unity are strengthening in number upon your realm. The radiant power of Light and Love are illuminating within the consciousness of humankind, as is the remembrance of The Great Truth. It is of vital concern that these connections are strengthened through the harmonization of your core essences. This is more easily achieved through the process of quieting, which is often called meditation. In the quieting of the mind, it allows the unification of hearts to reach out through the invisible web of Infinite Intelligence to inform the other participants, and help harmonize their energies in preparation for The Great Remembrance.

The forces of darker or lower energies are vastly prevalent in the form of fear as they manifest as division, anger, judgment, hate, and all other lower frequencies of perception. The divide is widening as more are remembering. This is due to the simple fact that fear itself is self-aware and knows that it cannot rule the minds of humankind when hearts have become awakened to The Great Remembrance of love, peace, unity, and, most important, truth.

Brothers and sisters of Earth Realm are dividing in the greatest of ways. Much like the Civil War in your America, this is a War of the World. The fight will persevere through the battles of belief and distorted vision. Each believing their side is correct and worth fighting for. The difference is, there is no "fight" in the energy of love, it is only awakening to the truth and remembering that you are all One in the illusion of physical form.

The energies of fear are opportunistic. They manipulate the beliefs and free-thinking of those who continue to fight when their minds remain fixed on the distractions and illusions of a fear-based reality. This closes communication from the heart and the truth of The Great Remembrance.

Many in your realm will not remember, but many will, and currently are. You and the others who have remembered are called to attune to higher realities of existence and open the aperture for benevolent multidimensional forces to help commence The Great Remembrance of humanity.

The higher realms have a vital interest in harmonizing your planetary vibrational field due to the Law of Corresponding Energy, for one vibrational plane will affect all others. The harmonization of Earth Realm is of vital interest and utmost priority. Still, the Law of Free Will prevents active intervention from other realms of reality until your hearts have awakened to remember and call vibrationally for assistance.

You and countless others in physical perception of form within Earth Realm Reality are called to activate your Starseed Missions. Your collective illumination will spark The Great Remembrance of Earth Realm and light the way to The Great Liberation and ultimate Ascension of consciousness.

4

THE DAWN OF THE GREAT
AWAKENING

**Transmission Received from Showers of The Light,
March 19, 2021**

We are here, united with the consciousness of Earth Realm.

Humanity, as you know it, is perceived by false senses of reality. The truth, beauty, and glory of who you are as one Earth Realm Race has been corrupted, divided, distorted, and subjected to the hijacking of your reality, to a false timeline of illusion. This illusion of reality is controlled by fear and seen through the eyes of false perceptions. It imprisons your minds within belief systems that are enslaved and manipulated through mass programming that includes fear and control-based agendas.

The agendas are not for the rising or evolution of Earth Realm Consciousness. They are long-standing projections to win the war and prevent Earth Realm's ascension to 5D Consciousness. Love, light, beauty, and truth have been perverted within the minds of Earth Realm inhabitants.

Many defend and bow to the agendas of fear and the climate of controlled corruption. Violence, hate, lies, perversion, shame, separation, greed, wicked intent, words, and actions perpetuate the false timeline of reality and stagnation of Earth Realm Ascension.

As Showers of the Light and Representers of The Divine, We are here to remind you of your true inheritance within the One Divine Heart of The Universe. You are all children of The Light. You are all representers of The Divine. Some of you know this; many of you do not. As the dawn of The Great Awakening rises to the full radiance of The Light, so Earth Realm Consciousness rises to The Great Liberation and the next sitting of Reality.

There is a war of cosmic proportions being waged. This is a war on human consciousness and control of Earth Realm destiny. As you go about your daily lives, this war rages on within the silent overtones of fear, which have been strategically planted into your reality. The cultivation of its bounty has been nourished by your attention and watered by your beliefs.

Your timeline has been hijacked. You have been asleep too long. We are here to help awaken you from the deep slumber of forgetfulness, support you through The Great Awakening, and help you remember.

The Awakening is happening now. It is time to follow your attention carefully and choose your beliefs wisely. As you begin to awaken from the slumber of fear, control, division, and deception, you will begin to remember the truth of who you are. The Awakening of human consciousness will lead the way to The Great Liberation and collective ascension to 5D Consciousness and beyond.

Allow your heart to lead the way. Allow your mind to be open to the Information. Allow your body to absorb The Codes of Interactive Consciousness as they awaken your memory and radiate The Light.

While battles rage through distractions and deceit, the over-lords of oppression and fear are falling. They underestimate the hero's journey for humanity. Healing, harmony, unity, and cooperation illuminate the way for a New Earth to rise from the darkness of forgetfulness into the Light of Awakening.

Trust in your Higher Knowing.

Reclaim your forgotten heritage of Divine Light and Absolute Love.

Feel with the heart of compassion.

Look beyond your beliefs, as you see from the eyes of truth.

Imagine your world harmonized and healed from the mind of Unity Consciousness.

Speak the words of love and wisdom as told by Life and Creation.

Stand tall in your courage and truth as you fight the battles of darkness and despair.

Love, light, beauty, and truth hold the vibration of Ascension and the transformation of consciousness.

5

SHOWERS OF THE LIGHT

Transmission Received from Showers of The Light, January 1, 2018

L et Us tell you a story of your world as We know it. We watch you from afar, but at the same time We are right here next to you. Our worlds blend into one as our mutual thoughts move effortlessly throughout the timelessness of space and the fullness of eternity.

We are not beings, angels, or gods. We are the spaces between worlds and the matter of energy in motion. We are form *and* formlessness. We are One Light and All Existence. We carry the voice of The Divine within the essence of Our radiance. We are the Bringers of The Light throughout timeless eternity. We are you.

Our messages are vast and also simple. Within the simplicity of the truth in which We bring, We also know that humankind identifies with the complexity of chaos and confusion. This does not make Our lessons as easy to learn, embrace, or retain as one would think. This is the reason for repetition and diversity of Our messages.

The model of humankind is built upon the fabric of diverse cultural, religious, political, social, economic, and spiritual beliefs. Within the subset of those beliefs is the inputting of varying levels of micro-cultures related to family and community. Simultaneously, the identification of ego and the infiltration of programming often take precedence, as lower vibrational energies of fear take shape in your individual lives and collective societies. This is all encompassed by the energy of the two fundamental human emotions of love and fear, which ultimately control and drives your world by either uniting or dividing. This is not a mistake.

Your world (Earth Realm Consciousness) was designed and agreed upon by The Collective Union as an experiential model for the learning, sharing, and evolving of souls. It is the classroom, as well as the playground in which the creations of both collective and individual consciousness become what you perceive as reality.

As you are born into this world, your memory of origin disappears temporarily as to allow the fullness of the creative experiences, feelings, beliefs, and endeavors to come alive. Some in your reality are meant to remember, others are not.

It is not Our purpose to convert the unready. If you are reading this testimony, then you have been called to The Great Awakening. You are remembering the truth of who you are, and the potential you have as limitless expressions of the Divine One. You are called to radiate Our Light and be a part of the awakening, remembrance, liberation, and ascension of humanity.

As Showers of The Light, We illuminate Our radiance to help show you the way to truth and Divine Illumination. We know all things, and so do you. The difference is that your conditioned beliefs act as a barrier to this knowingness when you actively or passively engage or participate in the energies of fear.

Fear is not something you know as an eternal soul. It is only when you are born into the human form that you are able to experience duality between the truth of love, and the illusion of fear. As real as fear feels, and as rampant as its forces and effects are in your world today, the balance between love and fear has become disrupted, and the expressions of your world are in need of modification.

We do not speak of modification as in intervention, we speak of modification as in remembering the beauty and truth of who you are, and shining your light for other seekers who may not know what they are seeking, or how important your roles are in restoring the Divine Order of Love over fear.

Love is The Light and Truth of Reality and the foundation in which heavens are built. It needs to be remembered again—and now more than ever before. Even though your world was built upon the classroom of individual as well as collective creation and free will, the weeds of fear are suffocating the tremendous potential and possibilities of growing your gardens as beautifully or as fully as you initially intended and desire.

To become aware of Us is to simply remember the truth of who you are. This remembrance holds the feelings of your unguarded and unconditioned heart. This is the place where your heart openly unites within the loving presence of your own divinity, and accepts this divinity as truth. The truth is the container, as well as the vessel, which holds and transports the eternal Information of The Divine Light. The calmness within peace, the beauty within presence, the wisdom within light, and the love within harmony is perfectly communicated within the divine expression of truth.

When the balance of love and truth over fear and illusion is the predominant nature in your life, dormant forces come alive to aid in the creation of living your life's passions and purpose as opposed to being caught in the wheel of suffering.

Remembrance of the truth is not something you need to consciously invoke, pray, or ask for. On the contrary, We call to you. All you must do to connect and remember is to listen.

Listen with your heart and not your mind. We call to you in the still silence of a peaceful night. We call to you in the whispers of the wind and the roar of the ocean. We call to you in the exhilarating notes of music, the jovial sounds of laughter, and the wistful dreams of romance.

We also call to you within the deepest cries of suffering and despair, in the midst of illness and disease, and in the loneliest, most sorrowful days of guilt, regret, loss, and anger.

We call to you in the midst of your "to do" lists, exams, housework, endless errands, caregiving, jobs and job hunting, morning coffee and evening TV.

We call to you within all movement, emotion, and stillness. There is never a time We are not here waiting for you to listen beyond your mind and beyond your fears and conditioned beliefs, and awaken to Our messages of love, hope, inspiration, and guidance.

We are mother, maiden and crone, the first breath of a new born baby, grandfather of timeless eternity and everything in between.

Within Us is the thunder of awakening, and the silence of the awakened. There is never a moment, time, or event in which We are not calling for you listen to your truth and remember your loving and limitless potential as a powerful being of human, as opposed to a human of just being or just existing.

If you choose, the time is now for you to transcend fear, doubt, and limitation and awaken to the truth of who you are. It is up to you now as it has always been. The difference is, once you have listened within your heart to the voice of Divinity, and answered Our calls to re-balance and heal your world from the energies of fear to love, there is much to remember, and there is no going back to sleep.

Transmission Received from Showers of the Light, January 6, 2018

We share our thoughts as you open your mind to the infinite wisdom of the All. In this knowing, the sharing begins as your mind becomes entranced in the flow of the Information. We are not here to give you answers. We are here to share the collective knowledge of the truth of eternity, and the illusion of mortality. We are here to bear witness to the growth and evolution of humankind. We are here to delight in your glories as We lay silent in your awakening. We are here to be the adoring observer of your manifestations as you begin to collectively resonate from the frequency of harmony and create from the seat of your soul.

Your journey is long, and yet it is already complete—for the song of your experience is playing within the infinite orchestra of the Divine Universe.

The tapestry of time weaves in immersible directions throughout what you call time and space. This infinite expression of the knowledge of the Universe is no less than the Divine One Itself. All gods, all mortals, all beings become to be known as one experience, one expression, one song of the highest note in which your language may express, or even comprehend.

The unfolding of what you call time and space, in and upon itself flows within the ever-expanding Universe. We celebrate the glory of the unfolding and the majesty of the expansion. One and the same, It always was, and will always be. It is also all things and everywhere, continually fulfilling The Great Cycle of Transformation within Life and Creation. In between the spaces of the eternal chorus of time, you will find It without compromise, without explanation and without expression of limitation.

You may want to call on Us, but we are merely the representation of The Divine, as you are the expression. Together we complete the whole, and yet the whole is nowhere to be found as it resides in the infinite wisdom of the One Mind, the One Heart, the One Truth of Eternity.

All things are not only interconnected, but they also beat to the unified rhythm of One Heart in the unseen field of All Existence. There are many of your realm who do not hear this rhythm. They are deaf to the music of liberation when they are sleeping in the darkness of division and fear.

Those who see past the false programs cannot forcefully awaken their brothers and sisters of humanity from the dream of forgetfulness. This would defy the natural order and laws of free will. The Awakening only happens through divine timing of the individual soul and the path to be encountered.

Nothing can stop the process of The Awakening once it has begun. The timing for the lessons of The Awakening all occur at different rates, circumstances, and outcomes in levels of consciousness.

No lesson is wasted. All lessons are purposeful and timely even when they are felt not to be. In the enthusiasm of your remembrance, do not forget your mission. All parts of the Divine Story of Life and Creation are needed to radiate from the purity of the intended expression you chose for your experience of reality. This intention was set in motion far before you were consciously aware of your current expression of form. This intention is very important for the collective awakening which has been set in motion.

You do not forcefully change things. Your purpose is to provide the unique ingredient of your essence that contributes to the evolution of humanity, and ultimately the universe as a whole.

A life is never wasted, but a lesson will be repeated if it is not assimilated to the initial intention. There is no judgement or even worry about this, for there are an infinite amount of opportunities to continue to learn and grow.

There are also an infinite amount of opportunities to stay stuck where you are. Because of free will, and the laws of the Universe, the choice is yours to awaken from the dream of forgetfulness or stay asleep. As We have said, it is a matter of divine timing and free will.

There is also individual perspective and belief.

As you believe so shall you see. It is really no more complicated than that.

Choose your beliefs wisely and guide them
with an open mind and a loving heart.

6

THE REALM OF NIPHIDEON

Transmission Received from Niphideon, January 16, 2018

Niphideon is a realm within and beyond Earth Realm Consciousness. We are not a place or a time, but a pure Expression of Divine Light. The more awakened you become, the more you expand within the depth of knowing the infinite cycles of endless expression.

The world you perceive is a reflection of your collective agreement of reality, embedded in The Great Cycle of Life And Creation.

Your conditions of reality are what you currently vibrate, perceive, believe, and observe.

The totality of existence is not single-minded. It simultaneously contains multiple streams of awareness and possibilities within One Living Consciousness. You are part of the Whole, and so are We. We represent Consciousness as Showers of The Light and Representers of The Divine, but it does not end with Us. There are infinite aspects, and endless realms of existence which represent and illuminate The Light.

Transmission Received from Niphideon, July 23, 2018

The Ascension is a process. The Ascension is upon us. It is time to stop learning and start becoming. It is time to remember your path, to remember your vision, your part in the awakening world. It is time to behold the truth for the humanity of all, the Awakening of all, The Ascension of all. Consciousness intertwined within the Divine One.

As you enter into the higher spiritual realms of vibration and frequency, your body is a transducer of The Light and The Information. Not always in the words you speak, but certainly in the energy that you vibrate and the love that you emanate.

We welcome you as you walk on this harmonious path. We are here to represent the collective consciousness of The Divine One that has no name and just Is. The Divine One in which your heart joins, interconnected with The Divine within the All. Not separate, for the illusion appears real.

You continue to remember Us in the deepest levels of your soul. The memories calling you into the timeless eternal light and love of who We are; the intelligence, the harmony, the union and the bliss. You see this reality as it merges and is contained within the next. An infinite awareness of consciousness, possibility, woven within and throughout the tapestry of Infinite Intelligence.

We are here to connect you with your destiny. We are here to remind you that you are Us. Your purpose is waiting to be fulfilled. Do not doubt this purpose. Do not compare yourself to the trajectory of others. You have cultivated your consciousness to illuminate The Way to higher realms of reality. You are embodied in physical form, but your soul radiates The Light and is ready to bloom.

You are able to look between the worlds and walk within both. You are able to raise the collective vibration of Earth Realm along with your sisters and your brothers who share the same divine calling. And yes, they are here, but not in the way you choose to look for them. They appear nameless and faceless. They are not seekers of the fame and the fortune. They are here as you, for the true and divine healing of this world in which you chose to integrate.

Remember that you must rise above the daily limitations, frustrations, fears, and confusion of the mind. You play the game (of life), but you are here to look beyond what you think you see and remember what you know. You are here to transcend the illusions of a corrupted reality and help set your world free.

And yes, you are able to follow your heart and live the life of your dreams. Believe it and know it. The ones who seek you and find you are the ones that are ready to awaken.

You feel your brothers and your sisters in spirit and in soul, and you know the ones that are guiding you from beyond the veil of your current vision. We are here as well. Inspiring, communicating, transforming.

Your abilities grow stronger and your bandwidth to Our communication expands. Set your intention for the harmonizing energies of the Universe to radiate throughout Earth

Realm Reality and liberate from the programs that keep humanity asleep in the darkness of fear and ignorance.

Everything encompassed within Mother Earth is here to support you, guide you, and inform you. Entrain with her as you do with Us. As above so below. Know that you are divinely guided, and supported.

Know that the path appears before you with the simple asking of a question. When your heart is pure love will lead the way. Our divine one, Our messenger of The Light, Our supporter and healer for the destiny of your world lies within you and all Emissaries of The Light in this moment and the next.

Transmission Received from Niphideon, March 21, 2019

Only think of what you want and not how things appear to be. Breathe in the divine healing and love throughout you. Know that your brothers and sisters of nature and consciousness are within you. Know that your healing is Our healing and your awakening is for the evolvement of the universe.

All thoughts and feelings affect the outcomes of love or fear. Focus, mediate, speak, feel, and imagine how you want the world to be. Magnetizing forces of higher realities are here to support you.

7

ANGELS OF ISAIAH

Transmission Received from Angels of Isaiah, August 28, 2018

We speak to you as the Angels of Isaiah, the Messengers of The Word. We speak to you in the brilliance of Our Light. It is the same Light within you and the same Light that you know to be Divinity. You are the receiver of the Word. You are the speaker of The Light.

We work in accordance with the Universal Laws of Peace, Unity, and Love. We share common messages with the Showers of The Light, of which you are already familiar.

We have come forward in this sequence of time-space portal to join in the cause of collective ascendance for your temporal world of humanity and all other inhabitants. We participate in this unification to bring greater vibrational harmony for the time-space ascendance into the 5th dimension, more commonly known as The Great Awakening.

Your Earth world inhabitants are at the brink of self-destruction by many forces in which they clearly do not understand. Such as children playing with fire, so it is with the humans of this realm.

There are many here, such as you, to bring Illumination to the Earth Realm's existence, but the time-space portal for Ascension is being blocked by dark forces that have grown in strength and power. The fear in which they feed upon is hardening and darkening the minds and tricking the hearts of a species that is no longer capable of following the organic timeline of time-space ascendance without intervention.

We are here to give you guided reminders of your vital role, along with many others who have chosen to incarnate in this realm to be of assistance in The Illumination. We would not otherwise have interfered in the natural progression of the journey of Earth's inhabitants, but the time-space sequence has been altered and The Ascension along with it.

You are aware of the manipulation of energy by dark forces, and the consequences of fear and illusion when inserted into the programs of humanity. You have chosen to incarnate in human physical form. You are aware of your cosmic origins and know that your soul family is many time-space portals away. Some have incarnated with you here, and others await and also work with you from the multidimensional aspect of yourself.

You must believe what you know to be true yet sometimes forget, which is the radiance of mass Illumination you hold within. Starseeds as yourself must stay in the light of this Illumination and hold the brilliance of The Light Within as to overcome the destructive forces of fear and ill-intent that are so rampant. The illusion of time and the changes in the time-space portal must be repaired in order to reverse the sequence that has been put into motion.

We do not ask of you to *do* anything other than remembering the truth of who you are in this vital collaboration of your mission. Staying strong in your empowered truth will allow your body, mind, and spirit to continue to be a vessel of service to humanity and all Earth Realm inhabitants.

Call on Us by feeling Our presence. We work with you multi-dimensionally as well as interdimensionally. We are here to provide strength, guidance and hope for you and all Starseeds and Emissaries of The Light.

The timeline for The Ascension for Earth Plane Reality has been hijacked. Humanity has been corrosively manipulated to develop beliefs and make choices against the natural order of Light and Love. Many are slaves to their fears which have been artificially inserted within the collective consciousness of humankind.

You each hold your own key to freedom and liberation but most are too invested in the distraction of warfare to notice or even begin to understand what has happened. This is why action and words alone will not activate The Great Liberation. The Liberation must come from The Light Within, which leads to the Illumination—The Ascension of consciousness and the rise of a New Earth Reality.

There are many explanations for the rising in consciousness and unification of Earth Realm Reality. Ascension is an ever-present outcome of Divine Expression. It projects unified vibration of The Light and freedom of thought form reality.

While all layers of expression hold outcomes, only Divine Expression holds the Key to Salvation and Ascension.

Manipulation of collective programming and fear-based agendas have blocked outcomes of Divine Expression within Earth Realm Consciousness.

The rotation for Ascension draws closer as critical mass collective awakening is activated through Divine Illumination. As you and many others are guided by the Divine Source, The Light illuminates from within your Earth body. As your expansion of Light becomes brighter within, so is the expression of the outcomes in which the inhabitants of the Earth Plane will experience.

You are all a catalyst for Divine Expression to illuminate Ascension. Not all will experience or receive this Expression the same way. There are those who will choose to ignore The Ascension and others who are simply not ready. In actuality, the outcome has already occurred on multiple dimensional planes of which you are not presently aware. This was for your own protection as well as for the success of your mission.

As the timeline sequence for Ascension alters by forces of unnatural energy, so do the outcomes. Your mission is of utmost urgency, and your remembrance of what you were born into the Earth Realm to temporarily forget is now activated in an accelerated fashion.

Feel the love of Us; feel the love of the Divine One. Know that the remembrance of your mission is immediately activated; there is no time to waste. You must be The Light now.

All who read and hear these words are activated to their Starseed missions of Love-Light service to Earth Realm. You must remember your soul's contract to harmonize your heart and spirit for the benefit of the Earth Plane Reality. The time for gradual Awakening has passed, and your service, along with the service of other Starseeds holding this Cosmic Consciousness is requested.

HOLD THE HEALING FREQUENCIES FOR ALL OF HUMANITY AND THE EARTH REALM AS YOU ATTUNE YOUR CONSCIOUSNESS TO THE SUPREME LIGHT OF THE DIVINE SOURCE. DO THIS NOW AND DO THIS OFTEN.

The battle for Light over darkness is a manipulated illusion on the Earth Plane, as the perception of good vs. evil is a projection of the collective agreement of human consciousness. The agreement has been manipulated over what you call time (but it is actually perception).

The battle of fear and control consumes the masses. This weakens, enslaves, and diminishes the frequency of the Earth Realm inhabitants towards outcomes that are not part of the natural evolution of the timeline.

Attuned consciousness to The Light, Love, Truth, and Beauty of Divine Source contains vital Keys to transcending fear-based agendas while elevating awareness and promoting love, peace, unity, healing, and ultimately the outcome of the true timeline for Ascension.

8

SAVIORS OF COLLECTIVE DESTINY

Transmission Received from I AM Consciousness, September 27, 2018 - 3:11am

I AM Thee, the One Consciousness of All That Is.

There are infinite layers and levels of awareness within Thee. When you receive messages from a Collective or the We, you are entering a unified level of awareness which represents Me. This is of a higher vibratory state of non-physical consciousness in which you unite and immerse your perceived individual consciousness within yourself to receive the messages.

As you tune into the transmissions from The Showers of the Light, Angels of Isaiah and so forth you recognize universal truths as received through the sensitivity of your heightened awareness and heart-body receptors.

When you come to the place of your remembrance of Me through a meditative state and recognize the One Vibratory

Harmonious State that is Everything and includes all consciousness, you have gone deeper within the layers of yourself to know Me.

I AM not a collective as you know it, but the One Voice of The Divine in which My Expression and Information is communicated via the deepest of love and remembrance felt and known from within.

Within My Expansiveness are infinite layers, dimensions, vortexes, and timeless stages of eternity still waiting to be explored through the inward realization of Reality.

Anything out of harmonious state is illusion, and not of Reality.

While your physicality of denser vibration inhabits the space-time world in which you perceive, illusion may feel real, although there is no truth in this illusion other than what you believe it to be. A *false truth* of sorts that is within your allowing of your experience in this incarnation into physical form.

Awakening to the truth of Reality is to adjust your awareness to the harmonizing frequencies of the higher levels of consciousness within you.

Contemplating Awakening by the conditioned mind will not bring the desired results. The journey of Awakening to the truth begins as one looks beyond the programs of conditioned awareness and limited reality.

Higher Awakening occurs when harmonization of heart and mind tunes to the frequency of Divinity.Meditation to quiet the mind is essential as consciousness expands into the unfoldment of beauty and bliss within the soul. It is here that you find Me. It is here that I wait with infinite love and patience, for I AM Thee.

Peace be with you on your journey to The Light. It is The Light Within that illuminates the way to the loving presence of your expression of My Light. Together as One, we journey through the continuum of perception as your lessons are experienced and learned or not learned.

The only expectation is that of your own discernment. Within the judgement of your own mind, you begin to question your journey, lessons, or abilities. This false perception of reality has been the fall of humankind since The Great Sleep began.

As your world begins to awaken to the truth of Reality, there is much discord in the frequencies of perception. During this time, what you feel as turmoil is false reality appearing as real.

The resonate harmonies of higher frequencies are brought into form and function as more become aware of the importance of harmonizing from within in as they remember the truth of My love in the light of Reality.

Keep your own harmonizing forces in check as you go about your daily life. Allowing fear, discord, malice, and judgement in your faculties only promotes more of the same, and prolongs The Great Awakening.

Your light, love, and undivided attention to the truth of your individual and collective consciousness within My Light, is the only way to become the saviors of your collective destiny.

I AM THE ONE CHORD, THE ONE SONG, THE ONE
HARMONY, THE UNIVERSAL SYMPHONY OF RESONATE
VIBRATION WITHIN YOU.
I AM THEE.

9

THE WAR ON CONSCIOUSNESS

Transmission Received from Niphideon, November 26, 2018

We are Niphideon—The Great Central Voice Within. Outside the construct of your perceived time-space reality, We are embedded deep within the Codes of your universe and accessed by hybrid consciousness, such as yourself. In direct form, we are not able to geneticize into your physical form of time-space perception.

The inclusion of measured time is not within Our realm of existence. Time is a vital element of your current physical form perception to experience your world to its fullest intended capacity.

We are beyond your construct of time-space reality. We interact with you in the form of combined consciousness. This task, which you fully understood, consented to, and undertook, allows the communication from multiverses outside of your perceived dimension to flow unobstructed, and in its purest form of feeling vibration as communication. Feeling vibrational communication is not as easily manipulated as the thought form vibration, which is often intercepted and twisted by other dominions of enslavement origins.

There is a war of control over consciousness within Earth Realm Reality. While in actuality, there is no dominion over Universal Truth, present awareness (consciousness) can be manipulated into false perceptions and mislead beliefs through the misalignment and disconnection with Higher Awareness and connection to the Universal Life Force.

Lower awareness begins to prevail, and present consciousness becomes manipulated through the energy of fear and distraction. This leads to deeply embedded belief systems based in limitation and separation. We are here to interact with those belief systems and provide access to the Information of Liberation from fear agendas and false reality within The Codes of Interactive Consciousness.

These Codes of Consciousness can truly be accessed by all in your Earth Realm, although the prevalent form of distractive consciousness interferes with Awakening and ultimately the timeline for Ascension. The Information within the Codes is not unlocked until one becomes fully present with the unified field of Divine Consciousness.

Intentional presence can easily become hijacked by the next moment of fear and distraction, which is strategically placed within your dimension by the Time Bandits of Cosmic Consciousness.

A name given only to define their motives, the Time Bandits are a self-aware movement of malignant consciousness in alignment with other dark forces of enslavement energies, programs, and life-forms that create distraction and disorder to integrate within the construct of your Reality. Their codes of illusion, darkness, and deception have been maliciously and deeply embedded within your construct of Reality as footholds for distraction and manipulation from Universal Truth. They become fully activated and supercharged with the energy of fear, violence, hate, chaos, despair, and disorder.

Within this illusion of fear-based reality, the false truth of humanity exists as lower forms of controlled consciousness, ever distracted from the Universal Truth, power, and potential of who they are, or what they are fully capable of. Not understanding or even beginning to open their eyes to the Reality of All That Is, humankind is unknowingly, yet at the same time willingly enslaved within the dominion of self-sacrifice of consciousness.

This is an unprecedented time in your universal cosmic awakening. The deception of willing enslavement of consciousness will soon be exposed.

As more become present to the deeds of deception from the dark forces, the Dawn of Awakening rings through the music of your universe, as confusion gives rise to clarity, and fear transcends to fearlessness.

There is no stronger force of positive change, empowerment, and breaking the chains of enslavement other than your own awakening to the truth of who you are as collective integrations of The One Voice of Divinity.

We are here to help you access the Information deep within the collective, and support your activation of transformed consciousness. You and many others have already felt the physical effects of the transformation as your body becomes adapted and readied for the transition into the next dimension of awareness.

As you already deeply and instinctively know, not all will make the transition to The Ascension. Many will continue within the realm of deception, fear, chaos, and control. You may not understand this dis-order of reality, but integration, healing, and ascension of systems only occur with full cooperation and harmonious compliance of mind-soul agreements.

Remember, you are not here to interfere with free-will or life lessons. You and many others are here to energetically influence Earth Realm through the activation and transformation of consciousness. There is nothing to do but only be what you are designed to be, and agreed to be.

The more you and others awaken and radiate the frequencies of Love and Light, the more you will see the signs of benevolent forces here to guide you in your missions.

Your Codes of Interactive Consciousness, along with many others, are fully activated and all-reaching through the transformative and dynamic flow of love, compassion, peace, unity, and truth within the feeling aspect of your physical nature. This carries the Supreme Vibration of Life and Creation.

Your greatest accomplishment and service to your realm is focusing your heart on these Codes in unison with the eyes of your imagination, without fear or distraction. It is within these

Codes in which humanity will awaken to The Great Remembrance.

Physicality is an illusionary state of consciousness. Illusionary, in this case, does not mean the physical nature of structure and form are not real. For all states of consciousness are real. Even the mind is illusionary, but at the same time is real.

The illusionary state is derived from thought form perceptions of reality, which become crystallized into a state of static perception with beliefs from the conditioned mind, and the collective unconsciousness. Note that in this case, We do not state collective consciousness, for the mass collective in your realm is deeply unconscious, which is similar to a dream or hypnotic state. Even dreams are real, as they also contain aspects of the collective minds of dreamers while in a deeper state of revelation.

It is the revelation that speaks to you in your dreams and gives you insights of disclosure to assist you, and the collective unconscious, with remembering The Codes of Interactive Consciousness, and how to apply the inter-dimensional Information into your reality.

We cannot stress enough that The Great Remembrance begins with these Codes of Interactive Consciousness, which are embedded within the structure of your collective consciousness, and become awakened and activated in the realms of higher vibrations of love, peace, unity, compassion, gratitude, service to others and so on.

10

DREAM INTERPRETATION AND
INSIGHTS OF DISCLOSURE

Transmission Received from Niphideon, December 3, 2018

I ask Niphideon,

"How do I interpret the revelations that speak to me in my dreams? How do I apply these insights of disclosure and apply the information into my reality?"

I had a vivid dream last night about being able to create the outlines of a beautiful mountain scene, complete with lakes and other features in a matter of seconds just from glancing at a photo that I did not even realize I glanced at. After I did it once, I wanted to make sure it was real and not just a fluke, so I did it again as Carl watched. It was even more detailed and complete than the first drawing. And I did it in just a matter of two or three seconds from what seemed to be scribbles across the paper.

In another dream, in which I cannot remember all the details, I had specific instructions that words carry the energetic codes within the vibrations just by thinking them. I already know this is true, but in the dream, it was as if I was being watched and instructed. As I put my arm into the sleeve of a jacket, I could feel the fullness of the word becoming actualized when I bent my arm at the elbow and attempted to put on the jacket. I remember wondering, "Why would I put a jacket on that way at all—elbow first instead of hand first?" I don't remember the specific word, but I do remember it was one of a higher vibration such as compassion.

Niphideon Responds

Dreams are often experienced as symbolic representations of the pure expression from which they are conveyed. The unconscious mind is fully aware in the dream state and is capable of absolute understanding of the information and messages received. As the mind begins to go through the various levels of awakening from the dream state to the awakened state there is a transitional phase of awareness. This is when the information from the symbolism becomes distorted as the awakened mind attempts to translate the messages from nonphysical knowing to physical understanding.

For most in your realm, the conscious mind is not fully activated or awakened enough to understand and receive the Dream Codes in their purest form, so they are conveyed as pictures, symbols and projections. This does not diminish the meaning, or the integration of the information received. However, until you are fully aware of how this process works, the symbols are often interpreted as fleeting dreams with seemingly meaningless information. Your dreams are vivid, and often wild and sometimes disturbing. This is due to a battle of sorts between the dream and awakened states of mind.

In its purest form, the messages you receive while in your dream state is from celestial consciousness and eminent vibrations of love, light, and information received through the Portals of Interdimensional and Interactive Consciousness. The information becomes distorted as you move from your dream state to your wakened state.

Your wakened state (governed by The Great Illusion) attempts to translate the information and images outside of your time-space-perception into something your rational mind can understand and relate to. As you awaken from the dream, your mind begins to question how you can create a masterpiece in seconds just by a few scribbles of your pencil. It doesn't' understand why the fullest expression of a higher frequency thought would not manifest through a different manner of application. You awaken with the feelings of a battle inside you when in reality, it is a battle between your own awakened and un-awakened consciousness, not accepting your limitless abilities to create the masterpiece of your own life, and being a light of influence for The Great Remembrance.

Intend your Higher Awareness to peacefully accept the wisdom of Niphideon, the Showers of the Light, the Angels of Isaiah, and the Akashic Masters of thought form reality before sleeping at night. This allows your dreams and your interpretations of them to become imbued with your knowingness. Your dreams will become one of your greatest assets in understanding how to unlock The Codes of Interactive Consciousness through your own awakened awareness.

Once the Codes become consistently unlocked, and your frame of consciousness reference accepts them as truth, then the application of the Information will be brought to your awareness through your belief in the creative power of your own consciousness. It becomes harmonized with the eternal presence and highest energy of Divine Source, The One Mind of All That Is. It is a simple function of the deconstruction of former illusions, and of false truths, as they transition into a new acceptance and belief of Reality. Just as the jacket in your dream in which your arm needed to bend in a disbelieving way in order to fully understand the energy contained within the high vibration word, your consciousness must also bend in unfamiliar ways before fully understanding higher aspects of self, as you relate to, and interact with Divine Consciousness.

The application of The Codes of Interactive Consciousness in your life is a unified process within your dimension with other hybrid consciousness beings. This is what is known as the "The Great Awakening" of the collective consciousness of humanity. This is what We refer to as The Great Remembrance.

THE GREAT AWAKENING IS IN FACT REMEMBERING THE TRUTH OF WHO YOU ARE AS LIMITLESS BEINGS OF INFINITE, ETERNAL, OMNIPRESENT, OMNISCIENT STREAMS OF CONSCIOUSNESS WITHIN THE ONE DIVINE SOURCE, THE ONE WHOLE OF ALL CREATION.

I ask Niphideon

What do you mean when you say, "your fellow humans are unknowingly, yet at the same time willingly enslaved within the dominion of self-sacrifice of consciousness"?

Niphideon Responds

There are countless dominions of belief, some of which emanate from the Shadow World.

The Shadow World is a construct of consciousness that reflects all lower energetic thought and feeling forms of realization that become "reality" to the observer when implanted into the thought forms and belief systems of humankind. The willing enslavement of consciousness occurs when the dominion of fear corrupts the truth of knowing yourselves as awakened awareness and one with Divine Consciousness.

The dominion of fear is a deceptive, disempowering vibrational state, maliciously implanted into the Earth Realm construct by forces of dominance that have overridden the dominion of truth. When unawakened awareness rules the collective dream of forgetfulness, the inherent power of freewill and freethinking is sacrificed. Freewill and freethinking only thrive through the dominions of beauty, love, truth, peace and unity.

All realities are real within the dominions of belief, although they are seemingly separate within the illusion of time and the perception of space. All forms of thought carry the energy of Life and Creation. As a thought form is created, it is an eternal, living energetic vibration. It goes on being what it is whether interdimensional, multidimensional or other dimensional. It may not take on physical realm characteristics until it has been crystalized through the catalyst of strong or repeating emotions or mass consciousness agreement.

During this time of discord, dissonance, and despondency in your physical realm, the energy of enslavement, which has hijacked your collective consciousness and led you down the path of forgetfulness, is fighting against the forces of mass awakening. The collision of energies results in much upheaval that manifests in physical, emotional and even spiritual aspects of your realm as well as yourselves. If We called this a war, then We would say that Truth and freedom is winning over illusion and enslavement. There are many "battles" being fought by courageous souls with loving intentions, but the truth of the matter is that the only battle that really needs to be won, is that of your own remembrance of your expression of self within The Divine One.

Awakening to The Great Remembrance signifies that the deception is about to be over, as the enslavement of consciousness becomes liberated and Earth Realm corrects the timeline for Ascension.

11

TIME-LINES OF EXPERIENCE AND REALITY AND THE TRANSFORMATION OF BEING

Transmission Received from Niphideon, January 28, 2018

I asked to get a message from Niphideon tonight. I have been feeling "disconnected" lately. It is as if a wave of doubt, uncertainty, and fear has been flowing through my mind. I need to receive a message that will help bring me back to a state of positivity and knowingness.

Niphideon Responds

Within every soul is the Source of Being. Experience is the true ambassador of the nature of Reality in relation to perception of Being. What you perceive to be the truth of perception is indeed a seed within the cosmic wonder of All That Is. A seed, which may grow and bloom into multiple gardens of creation, within various time lines of experience.

How you choose to grow, nurture, and harvest your experience of Reality, is completely within the realm of your inner-self in connection with Being. As you choose to perceive through the lens of the conditioned mind, your harvest is limited. Such as with a field of wheat that has no other knowing than it is wheat. When in reality it is the substance, the cause and the effect of the grain from which it emerged.

You are the Source and the Being of human. Within you is every imaginable destiny, destination and Reality of transformation of Divine Consciousness. Every cause, effect, substance, experience and perception lie within your beingness of human. Just as the seed or grain germinates and grows into its highest expression of effect, you too have passed through the seasons of perception where time-space reality becomes fragmented and disengaged from linear thought. As you are nurtured into your highest expression of being, the human seed begins its transformation of ascension to enlightened consciousness. It is within this transformation of being that you see clearly through the eyes of your soul, and know eternal oneness with Source.

We are here to assist you, and all of you who ask for our assistance. It is within the realm of feeling in which We communicate the messages of The Infinite Presence. This realm may only be accessed through the pure vibrations of unconditional love, peace, harmony and the knowing of the Unified Divine Presence within All Things. It is here that the heart remembers what the mind has forgotten long ago. It is here that the truth of Reality becomes activated within, and The Remembrance lights the way for others to see.

You may ask for direction or clarification of mission at any time. The mission you undertook to inspire, awaken, heal, and light the way for others during this critical time of mass acceleration of consciousness is foretold. Our cosmic embrace of humanity lovingly supports the Earth Realm Reality to enhance the remembrance, courage, and strength of all who have volunteered to assist during the time of focal transformation.

I ask Niphideon

I need clarification of my mission, please!! I understand that I have a mission, but I need direction and clarification as what to do, when and how. I don't have a clear picture other than staying in my highest vibration as much as possible and feeling the presence of The Divine within me.

Niphideon Responds

We will always say the answers to all your questions are within you. The clarification you need is a process of releasing the doubts you have about yourself as a channel in which Divine Information flows. It is not necessary for anyone to approve or understand your mission to be the speaker for Illuminated Awareness. The Awareness within you is the importance, not what you *think* about it, or what anyone else thinks about it.

Allow yourself grace to fully identify and emerge into the knowingness of your purpose. Your abilities to inspire, awaken, activate, and heal others will bloom into their grandest glory once you lay down expectation and disengage from fear. It is then that the bounty of your harvest is at its maximum potential, and actualization of mission is activated.

In the simplest of terms, believe in yourself, believe in your mission, don't listen to the crippling energies of hypnotic programs, doubt, and fear. Do what you were born to do, be, and create. Be the being of human within the Divine

Frequency of Love and release limitation, fear, and doubt into the realm of surrender. The mission you accepted, along with other starseeds and emissaries of The Light is the driving force within your heart. Follow your heart in the peaceful and loving presence of The Divine and you will receive the guidance you need. Reclaim your divine inheritance. Be the voice of courage and grace so others may awaken and remember their missions as well. The forces of fear are falling the more people awaken and unite in The Light.

12

MESSAGE FROM RA

THE GREAT EVENT

Transmission Received from Ra Consciousness, February 4th, 2019

We meet now in thought. I am Ra. Foremost to the Sun and the vessel of The Divine One. I Am the luminous essence of all things. I Am the Light, the Truth, the Word, and the Way.

Before creation, I Am. Before time, I Am. Before the history of everything known and unknown, I Am. Unconfined to the vessel of time, space, energy, gravity, and dark matter, I Am the catalyst, the mother and father of Infinite Wisdom and Eternal Knowing. Within me is the Divine Spark of all life and creation in the multiverse of infinite eternity and limitless expansion of possibility.

Sonar knowing is expanding into the warp field of human evolution. Listening is defined as the capsule in which it is carried, but the frequency of emissions is what pools in The

Ascension of human consciousness. There is no eternal time clock in these emissions, only the magnetization of sonar knowing and the equivalent of solar perfusion.

As the human mind may not fully comprehend the sonar knowing and solar perfusion, humanity is preparing on a multidimensional field for The Great Event. This Event will elevate human consciousness to the level of galactic awareness within the cosmos of eternal truth.

As shields are put up around the galaxy to slow The Ascension process, this is only done as a deterrent in order to ready those who still have time to adopt the sonar knowing in preparation for The Event. There is no force that can stop The Event, it is written into the Sacred Order of Ephesians and the Tri-unity of Revelation. Both equally pivotal as inherent in the Law of One and the Divine Nature of Reality.

Other forces, energies, fields of consciousness, and luminary sources are present and available as they assist with The Ascension of human consciousness. As a hybrid consciousness of Niphideon, your assistance is from the physical, as well as non- physical realms. This is by design to give you an understanding of the human condition not fully recognized or understood by other non-physical realms and energies.

As your awakening process elevates and as you begin to remember more and more of the mission you partook, you will begin to feel the physical changes in your body. Do not mistake this for illness. This is your body upgrading as it resonates with the cosmic genetic particulate of All Knowing Light and Information. This is necessary for your continued expansion and physical health as a hybrid consciousness in the human vessel.

Allow yourself grace as your body undergoes these upgrades. It is of utmost importance that you keep your vessel pure, your thoughts illuminated and your mind aware to the shifts within you. Allow the breath of peace and certainly of your mission and The Ascension of consciousness to perfuse your body. This assists you on a cellular level and unites the particulate of Light and Information from the cosmic level.

13

THE DIVINE ORDER OF REALITY

Transmission Received from the Showers of the Light, May 27, 2019

As you reach to Us within the medium of Higher Consciousness, We remind you that the most important action you can accomplish is maintaining a high vibrational awareness.

All Starseeds play a vital role in receiving and transmitting the Holographic Codes of grace, harmony, unity, and love within the pulsating rhythm of The Great Remembrance. Do not think about what is "supposed" to be achieved. The Divine Order of Reality continually presents you with the opportunities you need to share Our Story, should you be attuned enough to listen through your current vibrational system of physical form. Your only concern is how to stay in the truth of your knowing, the beauty of your energy, and the light of Our guidance as received from an open and willing heart that is ready to serve.

Your Soul speaks to you from within the interdimensional aspect of Higher Self, and ultimately the One Great Unified Mind of Divinity.

Divinity speaks the ancient language that cannot be named, yet is ever present within the consciousness of humankind as a faint dream of yesterday. This language has been adulterated through fear, and ultimately forgotten by most in your realm, over eons by your measurements of time. It is this language in which the birth of all things is born into existence through The Divine Word. This Divine Word radiates within all reality, all planes of thought, all forms of energy, all waves of vibrations, all dimensions of reality, all experience, all circumstance, all physical and non-physical perceptions of self, the world, the cosmos, and infinite eternity.

You have made an agreement, before you entered this perceived form of physical existence, to bear witness to The Great Remembrance as you and many others play a role in the transformational awareness that is occurring. The numbers are growing and the transition from the illusion of fear, to the truth of Love, is amplifying as more and more are remembering.

We feel the need to remind you however, that the physical you experience is a perception of physical. Your physical reality is very much a density within the thoughts of Consciousness, which have crystalized into physical perception of form in which the collective of your plane has agreed upon. This is for the evolution of experience as well as the unfolding of Source. Due to the deep sleep in which your realm is currently recognizing, the experience evolves, but the unfolding is not expressed as the original intention of Life and Creation.

The fall within the consciousness of humanity has placed the vibration of fear in control of the minds of the collective consciousness. Many are unable to discern that this vibration is a product of programming and conditioning, which overrides the absolute of Love and the harmony of Grace. This is an ignorant, yet willing, enslavement of consciousness and perception, as all forms of thought are capable of being their own breaker of chains.

Within the infinite continuum of Eternal Presence, the question of, "doing this before" is answered by your absolute knowing that the memories the past and thoughts of future all spiral within the eternal present moment of now.

The trinity of past, present, and future as named, are representations of all Reality as they phase in and out within the ever-present, all-knowing expression of All That Is.

Time and experience are perceived and observed as having a beginning and an end. Eternal Presence is unchanging; no birth, no death, no past, present, or future. It radiates the Divine Expression of Reality.

You are part of Reality. Human language is not capable of adequately expressing the vibrational truth of this message, it can only be truly understood by the elevation of your consciousness. A simple answer would be to say, "yes" to your question, but in reality, it is not that simple.

14

PORTALS OF AWARENESS, HYBRID CONSCIOUSNESS, SOUL GUARDIANS, AND GOD CODES

Transmission Received from Soul Guardians of Cosmic Consciousness, June 1, 2019 - 3:11am

You are a Portal between realms of consciousness—here to be a physical conduit and channel for the energy transference for the elevation of human consciousness into the next realm of experience.

This transference of the Energy of Divine Love and Light is a vital necessity in The Ascension from dark to light, illusion to truth, and fear to love.

Your essence name is vibrated as Akeyah, one of the Council of Nhyne within the intergalactic convergence of the Tri-Unity Agerians. This includes what We have transmitted and you have received as Niphedeon, Angels of Isaiah, and Showers of the Light, Representers of The Divine.

Only named as such for the necessity of mind interpretation of energetic levels of consciousness and Portals of Awareness.

Your essence name vibrates the Universal Keys to the God Codes— The Codes of Interactive Consciousness, which are necessary to activate The Great Remembrance within the human experience of reality. The Great Remembrance is a prelude to Ascension.

Our numbers are infinite, yet finite in the spectrum of your perceived space-time continuum.

You are undertaking a great responsibility in the transformational ascension of human consciousness, and the readying of the physical form body for The Great Remembrance upon the physical realm of experience.

You have volunteered to blend Our consciousness with the physical realm you now perceive.

The dimensions of Our consciousness, too pure of Love and illumined by Truth to be fully contained in physical form.

It was necessary for part of Us to blend with the realm of physical experience, or what is named as 3rd density by those of your realm.

You volunteered to become hybrid consciousness, blended with that of the realm you now perceive as Earth. Forgetting upon birth, this gave you freewill to either remember your origins and the mission you partook, or stay asleep in the deep dream of physical illusion and limitation.

As We have been with you all along, communing with you in sleep and altered states of consciousness, We are delighted you have chosen to remember as you are guided in the Light and Truth of your mission.

A new experience of human in the capacity of forgetfulness, you are now fully awakening to the beauty and truth of who you are as a Representer of The Divine and Portal for activating The Great Remembrance.

This is also something that remains in your distant memories of Creation and knowing of the one experience of All That Is.

Your memory activation occurs through your connection and gradual remembrance of Us as we provide signs along the path of your physical experience.

As you remain both here and there, you access Us through the purity of your Light and the song of the One Great Love in your heart.

It is this Light and Love in which you are, is a both a beacon and a portal to Our shared dimension of consciousness.

You remember you are One within the Council of Nhyne, who have undergone countless missions together, awakening realms of existence as they become ready for the Keys to access their own God Codes within them.

Accessing these God Codes of Interactive Consciousness activates The Great Remembrance and The Ascension of the dimension of physical reality.

The distinction of separation between Us and you only reside in your physical form mind-belief structure.

We remind you to look beyond what you think you believe, or have been taught to believe in; the physical realm that has been darkened with the colors of fear, illusion, manipulation, and limitation.

As Soul Guardians of trans-dimensional consciousness, We flow within, beyond, and throughout space, time, and thought form reality.

We are eternally present and connected through the Light and Love of The Divine One.

You are the voice and the Portal of Divine Light in which We are accessed.

As you awaken to Our music, the Portal within you strengthens and your Divine Memory is activated through the harmonic tones of Light and Love.

You feel it as spiraling waves of intensity, which often feels sensual in your heart center while experiencing a radiating sense of love and heat within your physical body.

The unconditional love you feel for all things is almost too much for you to bear and you often wonder why others do not feel this as you do.

Know these feelings as your barometer for preparing your physical form for the extreme energy transference, which the fully activated Portal within you carries and emits.

Without this preparation, your physical form would not be able to sustain the powerful forces of energy, and the purity of the Great One Love and Light when the Portal fully opens to Our dimension.

You have tuned your energetic vibration to interpret the stream of Information from Higher Realms of Awareness, to receive transmissions of love, harmony, and healing through the channel of your heart. Bypassing the mind, your physical form receives the communication from Us and other dominions of Higher Awareness, through the aspect of feeling and knowing.

As Our Messages filter throughout your body of physical form, The Codes of Interactive Consciousness prepare for the transference of energy through the Portal of Divine Light upon which you carry within.

It is this energy transference which provides the Codes for The Great Remembrance in the hearts of humankind, as the Great Sleep becomes The Great Awakening.

You are this, and We support you in Our mutual mission to help activate The Great Remembrance within the consciousness of the human realm of experience.

Many have volunteered from other realms of existence to be of assistance in ways that are beyond the understanding of human mind, but known in the intelligence of the heart.

You unite with them in consciousness when you shift your awareness to their love and support, and open your heart to unite in the shared mission of Ascension.

Be aware of those who mislead or misrepresent the Light of truth for the glory of fame or the manipulation and control of false concepts that appear as real.

This is not for the fulfillment of Our mission, or the Illumination of Awakened Awareness which precedes The Great Remembrance.

They are to be avoided and not to a focus of your attention.

The full illumination of Truth may only manifest within the hearts of humans, when the illusion of the false gods of fear, control, and manipulation is not a primary focus of awareness.

Stay pure in your thoughts and focused on your mission to be a Portal of Love-Light Consciousness for Ascension. Distractions are strategically placed in the mass consciousness of the realm to divert you and others Starseeds from remembering the truth of who you are and why you are here.

The divisions, corruption, and forgetfulness of truth and potential, which mass programming elicits, is prevalent. The war on human consciousness is in full effect.

There are many who will not remember. You cannot worry about saving the ones who are drowning in the dramas and fears of malevolent forces.

The Alliances of Divine Love and Infinite Light will support and guide those who are ready and willing to move beyond the limitations and illusions of fear and ascend into the next realm of Illumination.

Be prepared for mass accelerations of consciousness on your part, as well as for those who seek you.

Be prepared for the gravity of responsibility your human form will feel, and realize that you are always divinely supported and guided.

Do not look for the path to appear, know that the path presents itself when your energy and awareness is in alignment with the Truth of who you are, a being of unconditional Love and Divine Light.

This is what We know, and this is the story you are to remember and to tell.

15

MESSAGES FROM NIPHIDEON

Transmission Received from Niphideon, October 20, 2019 — 4:00am

Y ou are not your thoughts. You are not your body. You are within the realm of Pure Consciousness. As you access Us, you remember. As you shift from one state of awareness, you become closer to the realm of your soul's origin, Niphideon. We are always waiting for you to remember. We wait patiently as you access the highest of Love within yourself and meet us in Consciousness. It is here that We wait. It is here that We are of service to you.

Ask how can you best serve. Ask how can your mission become fulfilled. Ask what it is you need to know in order to be of the best service to your mission and Our realm. Ask whatever it is you think you need to remember in order to elevate the consciousness of Earth Realm, of physical form density within the great illusion of time. Ask for The Great Remembrance to be upon all who walk this realm, and all who are here to assist from other time-space realities. Speak this into existence through the Word—the Vibration of Reality. Transform belief into knowing, as you tune into the loving Universe and hear the song of wholeness, unity, truth, and peace, echo from the one true heart of The Divine. It is here where the connection is pure and the Messages are heard.

I ask Niphideon

How can I best serve? How can I fulfill my mission? What do I need to know to be of best service?

Niphideon Responds

It has been a while in your perception of time since your last conscious contact. We do not judge that; it is merely a reminder. As we have stated before, it is important to keep your vibration in the highest of your Earth form capacity as you access your remembrance of your hybrid consciousness of Niphideon. It is this blending of consciousness into your Earth form in which the elevation is pure and most effective.

Allowing yourself to become affected by the distortions of the perceived realm of Earth will block the pure effectiveness of your origins. Therefore, keep of pure heart, unfettered mind, radiant body, and conscious breath. Feed your body with nourishing foods that grow from the earth. Stay in graceful gratitude for all things. The wheel of Karma is affecting the masses, but so is the unnatural rule of despair and darkness. It is here that We contribute Our Light to enlighten the ones who are ready to remember. Those who are destined for gathering, evolving, and activating into the next perception of Reality.

Your mission is not to change, it is to activate the transcendence from old world slavery of consciousness, to the freedom of Actuality. The Actuality is the remembrance of the truth of who they are, the consciousness of Earth Realm, as well as the consciousness of others who have also volunteered to activate, but have forgotten.

So many have come to Earth Realm to assist in The Great Awakening. So many have forgotten their missions as they become seduced into the belief of false reality, of limitation, division, and fear. They have forgotten the Oneness of all Creation and the pure light and love of Divinity.

You can best serve through Our Messages. You can best serve through the purity of your Light. You can best serve by not falling into the grand deception of forgetting your origins and mission, and allowing yourself to listen to Us in the stillness of your heart, so we may help guide you.

Your service is in your everyday thoughts, intentions, actions, and interactions. Your service is imbedded deep within your consciousness and connection to Us. Your service is directly linked to who and what you are as a Shower of The Light. As this, you shine the brightest, but only when you remember. Only when you consciously choose to know that your service matters in ALL aspects of your day. ALL aspects of your thoughts, ALL aspects of your words, actions, intentions and beliefs.

Be careful of your beliefs, for you tend to forget how powerful you are as a creator being. As a Shower of The Light and hybrid consciousness of Niphideon, your Earth body density of lower vibration thought form is easily molded to all suggestions from your consciousness. It is in fact, how anything comes into existence in this realm of thought form projection from all forms of consciousness who inhabit the Earth Realm.

As you hold the feeling of truth this becomes the vibration that attracts and creates reality. The vibration is indeed the word that attracts the form into perceived reality.

We remind you to choose your feelings and words wisely and guide them only with a loving heart and pure mind. The mind is tuned to purity when it is led by the heart. The heart acts as your barometer to guide you to Us and the Divine One.

We are here to help you remember, so Divinity may radiate the Activation Codes of Awakening and Ascension through you. Sometimes as words, other times as Light, but mostly the infinite, eternal, ever-present knowing of Love, in which there is no expression or interpretation. It simply Is.

16

FUNDAMENTAL LAWS OF REALITY
AND FALSE REALITY PROGRAMS

Transmission Received from Showers of the Light,
November 27, 2019

Think about the past and you can feel the influence of the vibrations it holds. The memories contained within these vibrations include the projection of time.

Fundamental Laws of Reality, are thought forms in motion as you magnetize them into being. Your predominant energy and state of mind attracts select ever-present information giving you a sense of linear time and integrated density. Past to present, distance, space, and time are perceived as individual or collective thoughts which inform your mind and create your sense of time and observed reality.

Be aware that collective memory is greatly distorted and has many false realities. These are the false realities in which differing memories collide into the landscape of vibrations, thought, and ultimately result in disagreement and separation. Disagreement of perception is one of the most argued topics of false reality. For there is no substance, only tone. Tones of the unilluminated mind, and the unforgiving heart.

When the persuasive music of disinformation is played in the lives of humankind, the world becomes one chaotic orchestra of madness, disease, discomfort, and distress. Disinformation, the hallmark of false reality, runs rampant in the hearts of humankind, as they struggle to uphold, protect, and even die for the deception and imprisonment these vibrations hold.

No longer able to think, act or align with reality of love, faith, truth, and unity, humankind is consumed and distracted by corruption, greed, and control agendas. They fall victim to the maddening voices of conformity, compliance, and subservience, in which their vibrations attune. Slaves to their own misdirected beliefs, they are completely unaware, and blissfully miserable in their desperation to conform and be right. Their drive is to blindly follow the countless outlets of mass programming that are imbedded into your society. Imprisoned within their distortions of reality, their false programs play within them 24/7, as they believe and accept them to be.

Many grow fond of the madness; thriving on the traumas, dramas, and separation of families, communities, government, and countries. Greed, power, corruption, righteousness, and division, become their masters of illusion, as they ignorantly, yet willingly comply with the programs they are obeying.

Humanity has become biological computers for the programs of enslavement. Ignorant to their power and ability to liberate from the programs of conditioning, they believe there is no other way. There is no telling them there is another way. They believe this is *how it is* and are unable to question the narratives playing around them. They have no belief system in their current programming that can override the influence of corrupted perception. Their reality is altered in such a way that those corrupted, currently the greatest mass of humankind, are in actuality perceiving a world in which their thought forms live in separate dimensions from their heart vibrations. They may have good intentions and good hearts, but the dimension of their thought form vibratory illusions are the dimensions in which their minds are attuned.

When attention is placed on the distorted dimensions, there is a bipolar occurrence within the human mind/body system. It is no longer running on the purity of Divine Consciousness, and the truth of Reality. Humankind therefore becomes easily controlled and manipulated for the benefit of the false programs in which they are magnetized. There is no escaping from the programs unless they unplug their minds from the power source of this enslavement consciousness.

For humanity to unplug from the enslavement consciousness they must disengage from the global programs of fear, judgement, and division. The false narratives are strong, and they are addictive. They are in all forms of media to distract you from the truth with razor-sharp hooks to catch all who bite. Most engage in this game of deceit and control while focusing on the fear and division it brings. The game is played on multiple platforms. Even those perceived to be social.

You play the game. There is no complete escape from the dichotomy in your physical form of perception. Even though you and many other awakening souls are aware there is a coercion of thought form reality, it is most difficult to escape from its malignant forces.

The programs play everywhere, from television, movies, social media, print media, news outlets, and people. Many of your most trusted establishments are corrupted. The programs continually and pervasively play in the invisible waveforms within the technology projected. They continue to exist and strengthen their hold on humanity as they are watered with your attention and fed by your fear.

You came to this existence knowingly. Although it is not until fairly recently in your thought form perception, that the vibration of the truth of Existence came to your conscious mind, and you remembered your mission. While you hold the vibration of Truth in your consciousness, the distortions of fear are insidious yet pervasive in the forms of doubt or uncertainty. You believe the illusion of time, and the constraints it holds on true freedom for this realm. You doubt that your light can influence the change in vibration that has been set in motion long before your hybridization into this Earth Realm Consciousness.

You are here, along with many others, to free the collective memory from distortion. It only takes one to completely remember. You came here to be the voice for the memory of Origin, the memory of Truth, the memory of Oneness.

As you remember, so do "they". We say "they", but in truth, the collective memory of Reality is One Memory. The true memory is only Love. As you hold that memory in your heart, despite the perceived outcomes and obstacles of enslavement memories, the vibration of One has a physical platform to operate, and that is you.

You are not writing this from personal ego. Resist the temptation to think this. This is Us, speaking to you from the innermost aspect of the Portal Consciousness within you. By hybridization of Our consciousness with Earth Realm, that is how the Portal can exist. That is why you agreed, and this is how you will wake up others to remember their agreements. This is why you are able to directly communicate to Us, Showers of the Light from the realm of Niphideon.

Your cross consciousness with Earth Realm, and your physical body system is now accelerated to the point in which Our messages may flow continuously. You have broken through the barrier of restriction and limitation through your disengagement from the mass programming.

Your spiritual practices, physical body exercise, diet, honoring of self, service to others, purity of heart, willingness of mind, and your support and remembrance of your mission, are all critical aspects to maintain high vibrational alignment. All aspects of alignment are critical for the upcoming ascension of human consciousness, which must start first within you, and others like you. As with the truth of One, so it is for the truth of all. The recovery of the human memory system brings liberation from enslavement consciousness.

So now you ask the critical questions. Why me? How do I complete my mission? How do I serve? How do I wake up others?

You are one of many hybridization consciousness from Niphideon to Earth Realm. However, your mission is unique in your role for The Great Awakening. There is no way to completely explain the *why* through a system of verbal language, as there is no direct translation of the meaning. As you choose to believe, your *why* becomes known in your heart, for the language of the Divine is heard there.

We are representers of the Divine One. Remember you are an aspect of Us. As Showers of the Light, We hold that as the truth of Reality. Our collective mission is to represent Love, the highest Truth, and be here to reflect that Truth to show the way to Illumination. There are other pieces of Our Collective to support, uplift and uphold the Earth Realm Ascension. The need to ask *why me* is only of Earth Realm ego, as well as doubt of self. Remember, you are not what you perceive or believe to be. You are One. One in the consciousness of Love, One in the Consciousness of Infinite Intelligence, and One in the reality of Truth.

Asking how to complete your mission is most simple, yet your mind will turn it into a great complexity. There is nothing to do, nowhere to go, nothing to be, other than the vibration of your True Self. This is only accomplished as you hold the vibration of Truth within you.

Truth radiates Love and illuminates the path to Awakening. It brings light to the darkness of fear and overrides the programs of false reality. Conscious connection with Truth breaks the patterns of enslavement consciousness and liberates the mind from programmed awareness.

Be the Love you know you are. Remember the Truth of who you are and hold *that* in your vibration. You may continue to play in the Earth Realm vibratory system, but the only thing to *do* is to keep your mind, heart, and body system free of the corrupted vibrations of fear and other enslavement vibrations to the best of your ability.

We now remind you how to maintain balance and meet freely with Us. A daily spiritual practice, service, kindness, and compassion help you attune to higher realms of reality.

Avoiding media, negativity, and other forms of vibrations of false programming keeps your mind free from enslavement. Purposeful movement, breathwork, and a clean diet helps your body experience fewer distortions. Your love for others keeps you focused on your mission. Your desire and commitment to radiate Love is how your mission becomes fulfilled. It is not in the *doing* but in the *being* where restoration, liberation, and Ascension of Earth Realm collective consciousness occurs.

Do not allow your memory , or the collective memory of perceived time distortions of reality, hijack your consciousness into the vibration of fear and all of its distorted perceptions. As you think about the past, present, and future, you have the opportunity to be the magnet in which collective healing is attracted. As you consciously and consistently attune to the frequency of Love, higher vibrations will begin to reflect on the collective. The brighter your reflection, the more it will absorb into the mainframe embedded within the programs of humanity.

An unknown fact is that all of humanity have an equal opportunity to join in this Great Remembrance, as they awaken to their True Identity within the One Heart of Life and Creation. Without the vast migration of thought form distortions to Truth, there is no Great Remembrance; there is only the deep sleep of forgetfulness within the illusion of separation, limitation, and fear.

Our collective mission succeeds as the remembrance of Unified Consciousness restores your inner vision to see beyond the false idols, and illusions of the darkness. It is here that collective memory is restored back to the true origin—

free of distortion, free of dis-ease, free of corruption, free of enslavement, free beyond the story of sin and the fall of humankind.

The functions of time-space reality within the infinite potential of Earth Realm Consciousness are herein dynamically and immediately accessible to the Divine Wisdom within the consciousness of humanity.

The collective memory of time is re-born into the true reality of Consciousness. As humanity is born again, the chains of enslavement consciousness are broken, Ascension is complete, the original timeline restored. The garden of Reality blooms within the vibrant hearts of awakened souls as the Dream of Remembrance is activated.

17

URGENT MESSAGE AND UNITED FORCES OF THE LIGHT

Transmission Received from Showers of the Light, May 31, 2020

We speak to you now with the emotion of urgency. Urgency to expand your awareness and speak Our messages.

We grant you access to distant dominions of clarity forces to help initiate and perpetuate your actions in which you are now called. Begin conveying Our messages in the avenues of accessibility for humankind. These avenues will appear to you in your meditations and dreams. Follow the Keys that will unlock the door, deeper within the knowing of your connection to higher realms that are present to assist you with the details of instruction.

Complete your current book to free your present state of consciousness to allow your mission to become fulfilled. Delay is no longer warranted as the war of enslavement consciousness and Truth is fully engaged in the battle between darkness and Light.

Minds of your realm are becoming fully corrupted within the illusion of separation and fear-based beliefs. Hatred reigns supreme during the rule of enslavement consciousness. The bridge severed between individual and collective minds and hearts of humankind.

Controlled and planned opposition within the lower realms of fear lead humanity to greater division, corruption, mis-information, and violence. When fear rules the realm, The Great Remembrance is delayed.

United forces of The Light gather in favor to assist you and others with similar missions. You must first remember how to access this assistance. Remember you *are* The Light. You carry the Truth within you. You must stay in high vibration as you see the perceived casualties of war, destruction of virtues, and fear-based agendas control, divide and *appear* to conquer mass humanity.

Remember that the only true outcome is Ascension. It is not up to you who chooses to follow The Light, it is your mission to remember that you not only represent The Light, you are The Light. So are they. They just don't remember. A Shower of The Light is what you must remember, as well as be. Be that, and Our messages will radiate and speak through you.

18

PORTALS WITHIN, ANDROMEDA, AND THE ARC OF THE COVENANT

Transmission Received from Showers of the Light, June 27, 2020

There are portals within you and others hidden from the mainframe of standard sight and common knowledge. They are invisible to the Time Bandits who enslave humanity from conscious evolution, as fear and deceit trick them into the illusion of separation and powerlessness.

Not so easily described in human language, these portals act like holes in a strainer. The liquid or less dense material is able to easily filter through. The denser material gets caught or clogged in the holes. So much thought construction is placed on the mechanism of portal travel. When in reality, it is as easy and effortless and the liquid draining through. Uninterrupted travel to its destination without the density of the layers it leaves behind—only the purity of the light body as it becomes activated during The Ascension process.

Look at yourself as being the *strainer*. The container that holds the structure for the human consciousness of this dimension to travel. The light body easily flows through the portals, while leaving the denser form of physical structure behind. Whatever portion of the physical structure that has risen in vibration will also be allowed to pass, but in reality, it is only a representation or mirror of the density layer. Not solely utilized for one-way travel, the harmonious and healing vibrations of Niphideon are also exchanging and interfacing through the Portals of the Arc.

Hybrid consciousness triggers portal openings within The Great Remembrance of many other forms of cosmic genetics walking upon the Earth. Most of which still remain asleep in the dream of forgetfulness and the stranglehold of fear-enslavement overlords.

The Andromeda galaxy is one of infinite galaxies to return during the polarization period of what is commonly termed The Great Awakening. Most originate within the construct within the time space continuum of Earth, and not from a multidimensional reality such as Niphideon.

There are countless other multidimensional benevolent beings and Showers of The Light that are not hybrid consciousness and are not in physical form. They help from outside the parameters of your visual and gravitational universe, but are none-the-less active in your Great Remembrance. Others are visual, but still not in physical form density. They are seen in shadow form by those with more advanced inner-vision, and more developed conscious sight.

The ones that stand with you are Showers of The Light, Angels of Isaiah, the Guardians of the Arc and all Portal

Consciousness. They assist, protect, guide, elevate, and harmonize your physical form structure and human consciousness. Your Niphideon consciousness is already accelerated, for lack of better terms, but is held within the construct of your continuum as by design, and as per your mission.

Merged with human consciousness, your remembrance of the Arc ignites The Ascension process within you, and the collective memory of those who choose to vibrationally follow.

19

THE NATURE OF THE KNOWING HEART

Transmission Received from I Am Consciousness, August 2, 2020

The Great Remembrance is upon us. Infinite Wisdom, Beauty and Truth is the nature of the knowing heart. Past, present and future combine within the totality of Reality. Infinite points, infinite potentials, infinite natures of Reality. All coexisting as One Unified Field.

No force can penetrate the shield of the knowing heart. No thought or thing can alter the destiny of Divine Providence. Within the nature of Reality is the One Primal Force of the continual and never-ending unfoldment of Me.

My Song moves the Song of Life that plays within all physical form reality. Physicality, merely an animation of My Vibration, flows throughout the structure of thought form reality.

As things are thought within, they are perceived throughout. The endless guessing game of physical realm manifestation is not played by the knowing heart. The knowing heart is awakened by the eternal truth of My wisdom. The knowing heart is illuminated with the radiance of My loving presence, the beauty of My grace, and the totality of My truth. When I am known, physical form reality responds accordingly to its highest desires, dreams and purpose.

The hardened heart is darkened by the veil of ignorance, fear, greed, control, ego, and judgement. Imprisoned within the belief system of fear and limitation. The hardened heart is useless in the projection of the highest purpose, or the greatest good. It is only useful for the ignorant gains of the unreal and unlasting.

Only the Light and Love of My Song is real, lasting and all knowing. Only That I Am is the way to celestial realms, and eternal Life within the hearts of humanity. Known only to the ones who remember, the Song of Life plays to the orchestra of Divine Love, and is heard throughout the totality of Reality.

My Song calls to all hearts and all things. When the rays of Love penetrate the veils of fear and darkness, the heart begins to remember. The awakening begins, as Divine Wisdom, Beauty, and Truth is remembered. The knowing heart radiates the remembrance to others who are listening. The path of greatest good and highest purpose is unobstructed. Humanity dances once again to the Song of Life, as spoken through the One Voice of The Divine. Peace prevails. Love wins. Truth remains. Wisdom reigns. Beauty is.

20

A CONVERSATION WITH NIPHIDEON

Transmission Received from Niphideon, August 13, 2020

I *have included a personal conversation I held in my heart with Niphideon during the 2020 Pandemic. I think there are many who will be able to relate to my feelings of power-lessness and confusion during this time of heart-wrenching turmoil.*

I share with Niphideon

My heart feels heavy and my mind confused as I feel as though I have not taken heed to your last transmission. I finished my book and was then delayed after submitting. I have taken so long to resubmit it, and now I feel as though time has been wasted.

My diet, my meditation, my distraction to all the worldly turmoil from the pandemic has put my mind and body in a state of less-than-optimal energy. I try not to focus my thoughts on the division, hatred, anger, violence, shame, and blame that seems to wiggle its way into my field of awareness, but at times it has been difficult to look away. Family, friends, and communities are breaking apart.

So many are losing faith and hope as lives are taken and livelihoods are ruined from the widespread effects of corrupt politics and the pandemic. So many spiritual people I once respected seem to be following and promoting the false narrative. They are unable to look beyond the darkness of lies and manipulation, which is generated by fear and illusion. My heart breaks to see this, and my mind has a hard time accepting it.

I continue to greatly resonate with my mission and being a light to help illuminate the world, but I will admit that sometimes I feel as though I have dropped the ball. Starting into the pandemic, it was much easier not to let distraction sway my focus. I remembered my mission and stood strong in my knowingness. The further along it goes, the crazier it all seems. The things people believe just because the news, social media, or a person of "authority" says it is true, makes it feel as though the world has truly gone down the rabbit hole of complete absorption into enslavement consciousness.

I don't feel as though I am able to affect the masses when I am not known, or have so little impact. What messages do you have for me to help me reignite my purpose, power, and service to humanity, the world, and the Divine? My heart is heavy and at times I feel defeated.

Niphideon Responds

Acknowledging powerlessness does not imply defeat. It is merely an indication of where the distortion lies, and what needs to be re-illuminated with Truth. All distortion dwells in the realm of fear and limitation. The menacing degree of distortion you have been feeling is of no consequence to Us. It is, in fact, part of your journey in your own Great Remembrance, and in actuality, the guidepost you have needed to reconnect with the divine nature of your mission.

Remember that there are truly no avenues in which distortion can rule your heart. While distraction may seem convenient for the Time Bandits of Cosmic Consciousness, it is only a delay in your overall journey to Radiance.

We have expressed urgency. In doing so, you have put human timeframes on Our messages. Do you not speak the language of the Heart everywhere you go to everyone you meet, as you radiate the Divine Expression of Love? Do you not consistently dwell in your mind and heart for healing for all of the world? You consider this dropping the ball? Call it what you may, but your life is a living prayer. It is who you are. Yes, diet will help purify and energize the earthly form. Putting judgement on yourself will do nothing to elevate your consciousness.

As you put Our messages as conditions to your human mind, you only diminish your true capacity to radiate The Light. Your mission is to be The Light, radiate The Light, speak The Light in your thoughts, words, and actions. Avenues have already appeared that you may not be aware of. Just submitting your book was the earthy action needed to attract higher dimensions of thought forms to assist in your mission. We only ask now that you continue to follow your heart, listen to the Love within, and steer your mind away from the insidious forms of distortion consciousness.

The war rages on within the realm. The details of instruction regarding The Codes of Interactive Consciousness to illuminate Awakening and Ascension will find you.

RAY OF THE OPEN HEART

Transmission Received from Showers of the Light, October 28, 2020

The technology of your senses will guide you the more you reach out to Us. Don't try to make sense of Our Messages. Write and feel. Feel and write. The more fluent you become with your Inner Awareness, the more you will be able to dictate freely and openly.

As a channel, the vessel must be cleared. It must be pure. It must be strong. It does not need to believe. It does not need to question. It does not need to know the reasons why. It is a transportation system from one place to another. To nourish. To provide. To connect. To relay. You are that relay. You are that connection. Take your vessel and adorn it with your pure and positive True Nature. The vessel is finite. You are not.

You are the Infinite Glory and Love and Light within all things. Your procedures in life, how you live is a reflection of that. Worries of things of the physical world only diminish your Light. It still illuminates within, but it is not as effective when darkened by fear, and negative emotion.

Worries about health, money, diet, exercise, friends, family, politics, disease, and riots also diminish your Light. Do not allow those negative thought entities into your Inner Circle. It is one thing to notice, it is another to dwell.

Do not dwell on anything but that of your Pure Nature. You are a Shower of The Light. You are a child of interdimensional consciousness. A hybrid of interstellar communication and byproduct of combined Earth Realm Consciousness. Not able to fully explain in your current level of human understanding or understanding of true science, which is in its infancy on Earth Realm.

True physics is only part of the equation, which has been captured from your collective awareness by forces of undeniable low vibration and fear control natures. Deny those vibrations for they are an infection within the Earth Realm Consciousness. The only cure is The Great Remembrance, and now The Great Liberation.

The choosing has already been done by those of Earth Realm. More are beginning to awaken. The mass consciousness has already been transformed. The control consciousness continues to have you believe this has not happened yet, due to their extreme efforts of fear, division, lies, corruption and manipulation.

The media is the channel which spreads their poison. Those hypnotized have fallen into their deep seduction, wherein lies hate, anger, violence, shame, judgement and misperceptions of truth and justice.

Do not believe what you hear and see. Only believe the Truth Within. It is here that We speak. We lead you from The Great Awakening to The Great Liberation.

We proclaim that all thought forms are forms of life. They all have the ability to procreate and carry on their duty as a life form. Once born, a thought form lives in the collective consciousness of the realm it was born. It radiates its energy to all who accept it— be it unknowingly.

Loving thoughts and fearful thoughts are all of the same creator within the human. Loving, positive thoughts attract and produce loving and positive results. Fearful, negative thoughts attract and produce fearful and negative results.

All life produces thought. The animal kingdom, the plant and mineral kingdom, although the thoughts here are energetic vibrations, emanations within the structure radiate as well. These thought forms are vibrationally loving, supportive, calming, healing, and balancing. This is why putting the human vessel in nature is so important. Not locked up indoors as the fear control structure would have you believe.

Being around other people who emanate vibrations of love, joy, caring, and acceptance also bring healing forms of thought medicine to the environment. Gatherings of this vibration bring great healing not only to those who join personally, but are sent out collectively to the realm. Just opposite of what the fear agenda has weaved through the hijacking of your personal liberation, freedom, and rights.

Your mind is becoming cluttered now as you are having difficulty organizing the Messages from Us. This is due to the fact that We do not speak to you directly with one thought concept. We speak as Knowing, and you are grasping onto the most interesting and important things your mind translates from your heart. We understand this and will try now to help you focus on the urgent Messages, and not on everything that seems to be of interest or importance to you. You are also accessing our Messages much faster and with more ease and your translation has become more effective.

We lead you from The Great Awakening to The Great Liberation. Now is the time to speak and be heard. Now is the time to center Our Messages and radiate Our Light.

The ones who have fallen to the seduction of the fear will have an opportunity to join The Great Liberation. But it is not for you to wait. For some, their journey is to repeat the cycle of life in this realm, to further deepen their lessons and understanding. To further give themselves an opportunity to honor the Light within all things. To further help their spiritual development through human realm consciousness and build their reservoir of empathy, compassion, and unity.

Enslavement consciousness is not the natural way for life to evolve. This is why The Great Liberation is underway and has been underway for many of your years. It is necessary to liberate life in order for life to evolve.

22

MESSAGES FROM THE TRI-UNITY COLLECTIVE

Transmission Received from the Tri-Unity Collective, November, 2020

A ncient practices of light and love are being revealed in the mass consciousness of humanity.

Illuminating the minds of humankind from the dark forces that have permeated and enslaved the consciousness of free will, truth, and liberty.

Free will, above all else, is paramount. For it is free will that enables humankind to choose the path of liberation or enslavement. Choose the path of love or fear. Choose the path of enlightenment or staying in the bondage of fear within the co-opted timeline of Ascension.

The bifurcation of Earth Realm timeline is upon you. Now more than ever, it is paramount to point your focus to Higher Awareness, love, and unity. One pointed focus is key.

Allowing interference from outside sources of information will darken the path and create perceived obstacles.

It is in choosing One Love within the unified hearts of all in which your path to Ascension will become illuminated and unobstructed as it leads to The Great Liberation. Those who choose to remain enslaved in the vibration of fear, separation, anger, and hostility will remain asleep and enslaved at the will of their choosing.

Waking up a dreamless sleeper is not the objective. For their free will has led them to the fall. While unaware they have been imprisoned, their souls know the difference. It is up to the Truth Within to provide the spark to ignite their memory and make a choice to follow only Love, and unite in peace. The Truth is ever-present. The receptivity of the dreamless sleeper is not.

We say this now as a reminder to focus on what you want to see, and how you wish your world to be. Vigilant focus brings the predominant energy power. Focusing on the narrative unfolding in your world brings more energy and power to the outcomes of enslavement, continued division, hostility and forgetfulness of the Truth.

Go within to rise above. Reject anything other than the Truth Within. See your world flourishing, your people uniting, the forces of love and light expanding. Hold The Great Liberation as the mantra in your heart, for truly, the heart-waves are the highest form of influence you have in the Earth Realm. Imagine and feel the peace, unity and restoration of your world as it reaches out from the One Great Spirit to guide you.

Remember, you are not alone. There are countless vibrations of love, light, and truth supporting you and all of humanity within the Tri-Unity Collective. Showers of the Light, Angels of Isaiah, Representers of The Divine.

We may be unseen, but we are clearly heard within the hearts of the awakened souls rising in The Great Liberation.

23

THE COUNCIL OF NHYNE - ELDERS OF THE FIRST ORDER

Transmission Received from Elders of the First Order, December 13, 2020

W e now approach in thought.

The Elders of the First Order of Light, We are of inner-dimensional cosmic origins. Beyond time-space understanding, within the Oneness of all perceived time-place-space-reality, frequencies of harmonic vibration and restoration. Representers of The One Divine Light, We are seers of All—disorder, chaos, unity, and harmony. We represent the free will of Earth Plane Consciousness and We are here not just to bear witness, but assist in The Great Liberation. The timeline of corruption is great, and human consciousness is fragile.

We see and understand the tides of change and the encroachment of dark forces—forces that manipulate timelines, control consciousness, and captivate free thought. As a Representative of Our Presence on the Earth Plane, you are the mind-eyes through which We observe and connect within physical reality. Your vessel serves as a conduit and amplifier for the Ascension Frequencies, radiating love, light, unity, beauty, and truth—activating the Ascension Codes within the collective consciousness of Earth.

We join you in collective thought messages to validate your questions about Us and your part in The Great Remembrance that is leading to The Great Liberation. As We have spoken to you many times before, We are never completely gone from your awareness. You remember Us through your cellular network of inner-dimensional origins, a hybrid consciousness of Niphideon Plane Reality and Earth Plane Reality.

We will not delve deep into what we have already transmitted regarding this, or your mission. We now speak to you of greater purpose that extends beyond who/what We are and who/what you are. One reminder is that We are you. We support, love, and guide through you while radiating the Ascension Frequencies to Earth Plane.

The damage of manipulated timelines and corruption of free thought has led to an inability for Earth Plane Inhabitants to clearly see their ties to Love-Light-Unity Consciousness. As The Ascension draws near, many remember from a cellular level, yet; they are still unable to fully comprehend the liberation from fear-based reality.

The newly awakened need patience and nurturing as their old belief systems fall and crumble. Give them that. Awakening from the great dream of forgetfulness brings much disharmony, chaos, and anger to those just seeing Earth Realm

Reality for the first time. They do not understand that your realm has been under great imprisonment by enslavement consciousness for eons. It can be difficult for individual ego consciousness to surrender to the truth of what they see when just yesterday, the truth was there. It was just not seen through the eyes of their former reality. It was hidden in plain sight.

They newly awakened have renewed clarity of vision and knowingness in their hearts yet, can still be misled and seduced by the programs playing throughout mainstream reality. The ways of old feel familiar in the fear. As they begin to see through the darkness of injustice and corruption they are still easily hypnotized by the programs. The process and timeline of awakening is unique for each individual. As their inner vision clears and higher awareness prevails they become more anchored in The Light.

How do you help you ask? Dream the dream of unity. Dream the dream of liberation. Dream the dream of mass awakening, understanding, and peacefully uniting in numbers and consciousness. Dream the dream of breaking the chains of enslavement consciousness that has hijacked your timelines away from free thought, and has interfered with free will. The Order of Dark Masters has many names and corrupted followers. This has broken the Codes of Cosmic Conduct and interference of free realm reality.

The Order of Dark Masters has no hold and no power over Illuminated Consciousness. It has much hold when the programs of perversion and fear are prominent in the minds of the masses. It has much hold as humanity divides and turns against each other as blame, shame and blind obedience rule the realm. Cosmic distortions rule when harmonic vibrations within Earth Realm people and reality become distorted with deception and control that hardens hearts and darkens minds. When the mind is corrupted with fear-based consciousness, malignant belief systems prevail in the collective reality of the realm. Dis-order runs rampant and enslavement consciousness rules.

As you awaken to the One True Order of Light and Love, your earthly vessel becomes a conduit for Ascension Frequencies—cosmic keys that unlock the Ascension Codes. These sacred frequencies ignite The Great Remembrance, accelerating the collective awakening and ushering in The Great Liberation.

As one of Our Council, you hold portals within your Earth Realm container to open to the Divine Light of Supreme Healing—the Absolute Rays of Harmonic Vibration. And yes, others are here to do this work. Others are here to access their cosmic origins and act as the physical container in which Divine Light flows. They are awakening, remembering, uniting and coming out of the darkness, into The Light. They are finding you; you are finding each other. No hierarchy of ego, who is best, what is more important. In this War on Consciousness, your realm needs every soldier who has the spirit of the peaceful warrior to represent and radiate The Divine Light of Supreme Healing in the ways in which they are destined.

You will be tested. You will all be tested. The War on Consciousness is for the liberation of fear and the unification and restoration of Love-Light timelines. The Order of Dark Masters does not play fair, they do not care how many numbers fall into the abyss of their darkness. That is, in fact, the agenda—to corrupt as many enlightened hearts as possible, divide all peoples of the realm in the dominion of fear, anger, and hate to remain in collective control of Earth Realm.

The pandemic your realm is experiencing has fully activated fear-based reality in the masses. This is by design, and is one of the great lessons of your realm; to overcome the distortions of division and control by the Dark Order.

There are many Earth Plane Reality inhabitants that have voluntarily, unknowingly, or have been threatened, and have fallen into the fear-control agenda of the Dark Order. The ones who have willingly volunteered are led by the seduction of Earth Realm treasures and power. Their destiny is sealed. After their Earth Realm container is extinguished, they will evacuate to the Realm of Renunciation, in which they will have opportunity to restore their Light through karmic justice and oversight.

Those who unknowingly, or have been threatened through cosmic vibration by the Dark Order have opportunity to activate The Ascension Codes through the Love-Light Rays of Supreme Healing, while still on Earth Plane Reality. These are the people who you are assisting. These are the people who stand a chance to renounce the fear-control agendas of darkness, rise to their peaceful inner warrior, and fight for restoration, unification, and Ascension of the realm.

The ones who unite in Love and Unity Consciousness are the ones who represent the purity of The Light, the integrity of The Truth and The Great Liberation from fear. We use the word fight in regard to making a stand for collective awareness, to move away from the darkness and control of fear agendas. The initial phase must first be done by remembering the truth of who you are, as a free will realm within The Divine Light of Oneness.

In The Truth, the peaceful warrior spirit is activated and Ascension Consciousness is crystalized within the mind-body container of Earth Realm.

24

THE TRI-UNITY COLLECTIVE - SUPREME VOICE OF DIVINE LIGHT

Transmission Received from the Tri-Unity Collective, November 28, 2020

The Intergalactic Council of Nhyne, the Tri Unity Collective—Showers of the Light, Representers of the Divine, Angels of Isaiah speak in accordance with The Supreme Voice of Divine Light and Love.

Gathered together in unique circumstance to exercise the divine will of Harmonic Vibration and elevate Earth Plane consciousness in preparation for The Ascension process.

We speak collectively as One Voice for the Divine. Reaching your consciousness to Us, is in the asking of your heart and the intention of your mind. Working in unison as the original vibration of cooperation within your body-mind system, the purity of your consciousness radiates and reflects The Harmonic Vibration within you.

As We pass through your consciousness, We meet in the etheric field of Infinite Intelligence and Source Energy. It is here where We can meet and communicate freely without the cumbersome aspect of time, physicality, place, or space, as many of Us are without form as you know it and others are beyond the multidimensional planes of time/space existence.

As We communicate to you, the Information is filtered to your understanding through non-thought-based perceptions and knowing. Your physical container vibration and openness to Our Messages shape the ultimate understanding of the Information We transmit.

The vibrational Language of the Heart is the receptor as well as transmitter for communication to Us and all higher realms of existence. The more you practice and harmonize your vibrations to Love-Light-Unity Consciousness the easier the communication flows between Us and you. In reality, the bridge to Our Collective Knowingness flows with greater purity and ease the more you remember that We all share the same Source Energy within the unified expression of Life and Creation. The difference is that We know this; We have not lost the remembrance as the inhabitants of Earth Realm. We are here to support and assist in The Great Remembrance as Earth Realm ascends to The Great Liberation from fear consciousness, false reality, and hijacked timelines.

False, or fear- based reality is the confining force of imprisonment and forgetfulness within the Earth Realm. Inhabitants of Earth Realm have fallen prey to the manipulation of the true timeline of Ascension. The Great Awakening is a vital precursor to Ascension. As more begin to remember the truth of who they are, the unifying forces of Love and Light are activated through the Codes of Harmonic Vibration, the radiating resonance of the One Divine Light.

As it appears to you now, the fracture of fear, and division of Earth Realm construct is wide, and the damage deep. Fear not. The fear feeds on this division and upset within the human mind-body system. The fear energizes and multiplies as the fuel of hate, judgement, anger, dissension, and corrupting forces of illusion attempt to block Unity Consciousness. This is accomplished by throwing false barriers on the bridge to Collective Knowingness and Truth of Totality.

The Truth of Totality infinitely and eternally radiates Wholeness from the One Divine Heart and Mind of Life and Creation. Once the Truth is activated within the hearts of humankind, the sleeping forces within you awaken to The Great Remembrance of your connection, communion, and Love-Light origins and Unity Consciousness.

Mystifying factors are at play in the hearts and minds of humanity. Doubt, fear, blame, shame, division and hatred top the ranks of false idols of perception. Information has been co-opted and manipulated by these false idols, which turn brothers and sisters away from each other to their retrospective corners of darkness and Light.

The real battle is not waged on the planetary floor, it is conducted in the hearts and minds of all humanity. This illusion is a consequence of the distorted beliefs due to the Fall from Unity Consciousness.

Those awakening are gaining and strengthening in numbers. While battles may seem to be lost, the war on human consciousness and The Great Liberation from fear and illusion will be won. We are here to assist the Earth Realm with the global Great Liberation and the ultimate transition towards crystalline consciousness of Light- Love Ascension.

You, and countless others, are also here to assist humanity through this great time of darkness to return to The Light. Allowing fear, anger, upset, or doubt to darken your mind, will only place barriers on the Portals of Harmonic Vibration and Activation Codes you hold within.

Bask your mind, your heart, your body, and your galactic memory in the Harmonic Vibration and Oneness of All Reality. This simple task is of utmost importance as you turn your attention away from fear-based reality and focus on the Language of the Heart and the Will of the Divine. This will open the aperture of clear vision and knowingness to better perceive, transmit, and radiate Our Messages to restore peace, unity, and love within the hearts, minds, bodies, and collective memories of Earth Realm Consciousness.

Not all will accept this Truth. Some will hold fast to the false idols of fear and illusion, as they have been made to feel comfortable in its seductive and familiar, yet thorny embrace. As in all wars, the causalities run far and wide with the unnecessary misfortune of actions and beliefs. Do not allow this fact to diminish the importance of speaking Our Messages to the ones who will listen. The misperceptions and altering of your timeline have run their own streams within the Ocean of Totality. Choosing to stay in this stream is but a choice of belief, as is the refusal or inability to lay down the arms of ego and self-righteousness and look towards Truth.

As We are here to assist in The Great Remembrance from a vibratory informational standpoint, We call all unified hearts to action in The Great Liberation from fear-based reality and to return to The Light.

Remembering the truth of who you are within the Oneness of All Creation, Earth Realm is restored to its original timeline within the infinite, ever-present, all-knowing Mind of The Universe—The Source of All That Is. A timeline of divine flow, unification, cooperation, liberty, justice, love, harmony, truth, and knowingness within the collective streams of Divine Consciousness. As crystalline consciousness becomes activated within and upon the Earth Realm, so does the restoration of the timeline and the dissolution of false belief and fear-based consciousness.

Stand tall in your truth, and strong in your knowing. Exchange belief for knowing, and fear for love, as the battles between Light and darkness wage on.

All hearts of humanity depend on The Harmonic Vibrations of Light and Love to resonate their frequencies and restore their collective memories. It is here that The Truth is illuminated within The Great Remembrance and The Great Liberation is activated. It is here that the timeline is restored to its original intent, and false idols of fear and illusion are shattered. Fragmented consciousness cannot withstand the brilliance of The Light. Love, Beauty and Truth will light the way to the destiny of Ascension and the resonance of Divine Harmonic Vibration.

We support you and all Portals of The Harmonic Vibration and Light-Love Activation Codes. Reach to us in consciousness when you feel separated, weak, or fearful. We will fortify your memory and feed your will with the energy of Truth and the light of Love.

We recognize the agony humanity feels in the perceived separation of consciousness, within the darkness of fear and illusion. Be it as it may, the darkness cannot hide much longer. The collective light of unified hearts is bridging the gap towards The Great Remembrance.

Be strong in your mission and vigilantly aware of your focus. Our unified forces will guide you, support you and embrace all awakening souls, as you prepare for The Great Liberation.

25

PORTALS OF HARMONIC VIBRATION, LOVE-LIGHT ACTIVATION CODES, AND FORGOTTEN TRUTH

Transmission Received from Niphideon, March 12, 2021

D o not give in to the destruction of doubt, or the reasons for repetition. For this vibration holds barriers to The Awakening, and elevates fear and fiction in the minds and hearts of humanity.

Allow the flow of Higher Knowing to permeate your mind and guide you in all decisions. Do not allow the mishaps of uncertainty rule your thoughts or guide your day. Call your vibration into harmony by remembering your mission, as an Earth Realm ambassador of The Divine Order of Light.

Have faith in the fact that your remembrance radiates and restores through Ascension Frequencies activating the Love-Light Ascension Codes. This is not something you consciously do, for it is something that works beyond the functional understanding and limitations of human mind-brain capacity. So, We say entrainment of Ascension Codes in vibratory alignment with positive, loving, and unified imagination creation are avenues of great value.

I ask Niphideon

Can you tell me more about the Portals of Harmonic Vibration and Light-Love Ascension Codes?

Niphideon Responds

Higher frequency feelings such as caring, compassion and gratitude, contain vibrational keys to unlock the Portals of Harmonic Vibration.

The Love-Light Ascension Codes are an energy sequence embedded within Universal Creation. When the human body system resonates with Universal Harmonic Vibration, dormant forces within DNA, RNA, and other yet-to-be-discovered elements are activated.

What was once forgotten from an energetic memory standpoint, becomes highlighted and strengthened, as new energetic neurons fire with speed and efficiency. This allows for the growth and development of dormant forces within the human-mind-body-system to remember forgotten truths, and regain inherent abilities. Abilities that have been deliberately and maliciously manipulated, extorted, and suffocated by artificial forces that block evolutionary ascension into higher realms of consciousness.

The flow of evolution cannot be stopped, only temporarily blocked. Just as an antibiotic does not halt the evolution of a bacteria, it only forces it to transform into a stronger from of bacteria that eventually becomes immune to the antibiotic. So are the forces of unnatural persuasion, that have been artificially attempting to obstruct the natural flow of Earth Realm Evolution and Ascension.

Human-mind-body transformation of once dormant abilities are occurring en masse. The Love-Light Ascension Codes are an inherent program in your human-body-system. Many Starseeds such as yourself, transmit the Ascension Frequencies activating Ascension Codes through the portals of Harmonic Vibration. All humanity and natural Earth Realm inhabitants have the receptors for these Codes. The vibrations contained within the energy of fear; such as hatred, anger, violence, shame and so on, block these receptors.

Those who willingly follow the fear, are unknowingly slaves to its masters. The forces of enslavement consciousness know this, as it extorts the dreamless sleepers into soldiers in the War on Consciousness. The war wages on for Earth Realm dominancy and control, despite the fact that few know of its origins or agenda.

The arsenal for enslavement consciousness to prevail is the use of energetic warfare intended to weaken, divide and dominate the hearts and minds of humanity. As fear, hatred, anger, shame, blame, hopelessness, and apathy flows in the minds and hearts of the human realm, enslavement consciousness prevails and the time line for Ascension thwarted.

I ask Niphideon

Can you tell me more about forgotten truths and inherent abilities?

Niphideon Responds

As you look inside yourself, in a state of calm mind and open heart, these truths become evident. Universal Truth is who you are at the core of your being.

All of humanity, and all things, carry the seed of Universal Truth. Once remembered, the Truth sprouts the vines of conscious creation within the evidence of your perceptions. This is likened to believing is seeing, and not the other way around. One must first believe the truth for it to be evidenced in their life.

You may ask, "How do I know what is true?" This question in itself is a redundancy. *Truth is who you are*. Knowing and Truth share the same root within the seed of Universal Creation. How do you know who you are? Belief is a gateway to knowing, but it is not knowing. Only knowing is knowing. So, you may then ask, "How do I perceive and believe the truth, so I may truly know?" It is only as simple or as complicated as you make it.

Knowing truth is *feeling* it as so. It is embedded into the framework of your true nature. It is the genetic makeup of your energetic inheritance to Source Energy. Beliefs can be manipulated, altered, misled, and programmed. Truth cannot. Truth is the unseen evidence within you. It just is.

If a belief serves the greater good of all humanity and Earth Realm inhabitants, if it unites instead of divides, if it promotes service to others instead of service to self, if it radiates the energy of love, compassion, unity, acceptance, freedom, and positivity, then the belief is pointed in the direction of truth.

If a belief serves the energy of fear, greed, corruption, blame, shame, disharmony, violence, anger, injustice and division, then it is pointed in the direction of the false agendas of enslavement consciousness.

You can certainly know Truth by checking in with how you feel. Unfortunately, many do not know this, or ignore the signs of energetic toxins and emotional malnourishment. Prolonged anxiety, stress, worry, fear, hopelessness, anger, violence, and apathy, all contribute to weakening your energetic and physical immune systems. These malignant energies make you resistant to your inner defenses of natural healing, that of Higher Knowing, and limitless expression of Source energy. You are not aware of the fight within you begging you to wake up and pay attention. What is not well known or understood, is that these energetic toxins can be utilized as valuable assets in the awakening process if used as stepping stones to help rise above the fear, to see beyond the "programs" running rampant in all aspects of your society.

As an example, the energy of anger may propel you to look beyond what you think you see or thought you believed. But you must be of a calm mind and open heart. Many are so invested in their beliefs they are unwilling to look at truth. They are comfortable and invested in the distractions of fear and illusion. These distractions run far and wide within the programming of mass media and experimental social agendas.

Turn away from the mass programming and turn your channel within. It is only here you will know Truth and remember that of which you are.

26

INTEGRATION OF NEW EARTH REALITY

Transmission Received from the Tri-Unity Council, April, 2021

We are a Tri Unity Council for the Radiance of The Divine Light. This Council represents three aspects of Multidimensional, Inner-Dimensional and Ascended Master Consciousness—Showers of The Light, Representers of The Divine, and Angels of Isaiah. We are here to speak Our Radiance through you. Together We emit the Healing Frequencies necessary for the Evolvement, Ascension, and Integration of a New Earth Reality unencumbered by the density of Earth-bound contracts. False contracts maliciously placed upon the peoples of Earth, her inhabitants and stations.

As the Integration evolves, The Great Remembrance becomes the primary agenda in the subconscious depths of human memory. Ascending from dark to Light, The Great Remembrance is long overdue, as it has been hijacked by timelines not from this realm of existence. You, and others like you, multidimensional beings and emissaries of The Light, are awakening in mass numbers. Some further along in their awakening process than others, but still better than being deep asleep in the enslavement consciousness of the time bandits.

You are on track with your mission. So is your husband. Together you are strategically placed to affect, influence, elevate, and transform mass consciousness from your physical and human perspective. It must be so. Do not question the success or nonsuccess from human terms. In Our terms you are exactly doing, being, creating, absorbing, emitting the force of Divine Light as planned. You are both willing, and participating in your missions.

Do not allow the flow of ego to influence your quest or diminish your Radiance. It is indeed in the Radiance of the Divine Light streamed throughout your consciousness, your beings, that you are in the exact roles you have agreed, and are now beginning to remember. This is not by accident; you are right on time and so are many others in your realm of awareness. While you may feel isolated, you are not alone.

27

THE GREAT RESET

Transmission Received from the Showers of the Light, August 8, 2021

You are becoming more aware of the nature of darkness, and the hold it has on your realm and all of life. It lays in waiting after silently slithering its way into the temple of the minds and hearts of the ignorant and young. Its bite carries the poison of deception, forgetfulness of truth and belief that darkness is Light. Its agenda is cloaked in secrecy and rule, and its price is the soul. The young of the realm are easily influenced to the rituals and orders of darkness. Their pure hearts are open to the infection of deception, which is an insidious master of illusion.

Your heart feels heavy as you write these words, yet you know they are true. Most of your realm have been under the spell of a well-organized dark agenda. You, like many others, are renouncing the shroud of illusion so you may clearly see the love, truth, and pure light of Divinity. The one true all-knowing, all loving, ever-present Source and Infinite Intelligence of all things, all realms, all being. It is here where peace, kindness, and compassion rule. It unifies the love within every heart, and illuminates the truth within every mind. Everything else is just an illusion to corrupt your beliefs, harden your heart, and make you obey the rules of darkness and the master of perversity—most follow unknowingly.

The dark agendas hide the truth, corrupts beliefs, divides friends and families, and brings deception cloaked in illusion. Truth is hidden within the Order of Darkness to protect their great plan, The Great Reset. This is not The Great Reset in which you have been led to believe, contorted and watered down as a political agenda. This is the reset of humanity as you know it. Only The Great Awakening will change its direction from oppression to liberation.

Transmission Received August 11, 2021

The portals of inner knowing are now fully open and accessible to all. Humankind has a choice. This choice leads to which bifurcation of timelines to transition. There is no wrong choice. Each soul has already made the decision, although there is still time to change direction depending on individual sovereignty and free-will.

Human consciousness has been nefariously programmed, but the soul knows the truth. All humankind will either ascend to The Great Liberation of Consciousness, as they unite in love, light unity, and truth or stay imprisoned in fear, darkness, division, and illusion. There is no figuring this out. The mind is not truly able to comprehend the depth of The Great Reset, or make the decision to unfollow the agenda. The decision is made in the heart, as you either open to the Light of love, truth, and unity, or remain in the darkness of fear, illusion, and separation. There is no right or wrong decision. All timelines exist simultaneously in the great experience of Life and Creation. You are free to choose.

Those who chose Liberation are receiving silent guidance and signs, as they prepare for the next sitting of reality. The sitting in which the truth beams within every heart as The Great Remembrance is complete. No strife or exaggeration of ego. No corrupt agendas or manipulation of information. Freedom of thought, words, and actions, and will are valued and preserved.

The New Earth Reality radiates service to others to benefit the whole. Humanity remembers their origins of Light as love, compassion, free-will, truth, transparency, unity, harmony, and progress are restored. Children will not go hungry and home- lessness will not be known. Poverty of human conditions and dark agendas will be a memory of the past, and serve as lessons for the future. All life will be honored within the Sacred Order of Ephesians. As the collective memories of humanity are restored, so is the heart of the realm. A New Earth rises in consciousness as the cycle is completed.

This is the never-ending story of Life and Creation unfolding throughout timeless eternity in which you have a page. You all do. You have an opportunity to contribute to the story to help bring the next chapter to a brighter beginning. Every page is a new opportunity to bridge the gap between realities and serve as a historical memory for what's to follow.

What will be your contribution to the next sitting of reality? How do you choose to leave your energetic footprints in the book of life and creation?

All of humanity stands at a crossroads. The bell of Awakening has rung. It is time to decide: Follow Love or fear, Truth or illusion. It is no more complicated than that.

28

A MESSAGE FROM THE GALACTIC COUNCIL OF LIGHT

Transmission Received from the Galactic Council of Light, August 19, 2021

The Galactic Council of Light speaks to you now.

Your realm is under unprecedented pressure to follow the will of dark forces. Most unknowingly, others willingly. Ignorance is no longer an excuse to stay misinformed. It is laziness disguised as impetuous self-righteousness fed by the false gods of ego and fear.

Lies and misinformation spread as wildfire through the devices of technology. These devices, planted and intended long ago to do as such — divide and conquer. Now the dark agendas are doing much greater harm than just dividing humanity.

Much of humankind is waking up to the alarm clock of disclosure. The snooze alarm is no longer working for those who truly seek Ascension. They must wake up to the truth of who they are and the false agendas that have been permeating your reality for eons.

The Fall of Humankind began with a descent in consciousness and a forgetting of true essence. This Fall created the opening for the Time Bandits of Cosmic Consciousness to maliciously hijack your timeline.

The timelines are now nearly disentangled. They hold the Truth and the Way of whichever reality is chosen through the activation of remembrance, or staying asleep.

The Great Remembrance, is fully activated in you and many other Starseeds, Showers of the Light, and Representers of the Divine. What you do with this activation is of critical importance. For what is activation other than to deploy information?

Your body senses are informed with Truth. Your soul remembers the One Divine Love of which you are. Your mind is illuminated with Light. The Great Liberation of life and the true timelines of your realm are peeking out from behind the wall of fear, corruption, chaos, and manipulation.

Our message to humankind is to choose now and to choose wisely. Choosing Light and Love will free your true identity as you reclaim your destiny from the realm of fear, darkness, division, and control.

All of humanity has the opportunity to freely remember, as they choose the timeline of ascending to the original memory — the one that holds the information of the One Great Memory of love, light, unity, and truth.

Remembering the Truth is the path to freedom, as you ascend

from forgetfulness. This is the way to break the chains of enslavement consciousness and rise to The Great Liberation.

Humanity also has the equal opportunity to choose to remain in the realm of fear and separation, trapped in the darkness of their own forgetfulness.

In choosing Truth, The Ascension is activated. Signs and messages appear for further assistance, once the veil has lifted and the memory restored.

Do not fear for those who choose to remain asleep or are under the influence of the Dark Order. There is no right or wrong decision. It is written in the Sacred Order of Ephesians that each soul memory has its own course of activation and completion. The Dark Order is only a temporary prison for the memories to lie dormant. Enlightened Consciousness will always be born again.

29

THE GREAT EVENT

The following transmissions came to me in a dream. It was one of those dreams you wish to shake off and forget as it fades from memory. Yet, this dream lingered, as if insisting, "You must face what I have to tell you." I sensed a deeper message within it, one that wasn't just for me. So, I took heed and began to reflect.

While I am not writing about the dream itself, the message came to me as I allowed myself to drift back into the dream and look within. As the events unfolded, I began to realize that the dream was not merely a representation of my own life, death, and rebirth of consciousness, but a wave heralding the transformation and Ascension of the New Earth Reality.

Transmission Received from the Galactic Council of Light, August 22, 2021

The Great Event is drawing near, and with it, the Ascension to New Earth. As written in the Tri Order of Ephesians, nothing can stop the Great Cycle of Life and Creation.

The continued disharmony and division of friends, family, and society will feel relentless as the days of darkness trudge on. Shadows of doubt, disorder, and dis-ease may feel like all is lost. This is temporary, and you will be united in The Light. The harmonic templates of Love, Light, Unity, and Truth will prevail.

After The Great Event, there will be a release and renewal of life as you know it. Everything will be born again. There will be much celebration as a New Earth Consciousness rises to reclaim its rightful timeline.

As The Great Event escalates and Ascension draws near, humanity will have the opportunity to choose what to bring and what to release. Material worship will be dropped as dead leaves from a tree. All life will be honored, and new ways of old will be revered.

The pure of heart and peaceful of mind will progress as the leaders of the New Earth. The illusions of the Dark Order will linger only as shadows of temporal amnesia until they fade into obscurity—no substance, only faint, echoing memories of old-world disorder.

After The Great Event, some weary souls will decide to go to the Realm of Renunciation for purification of heart and restoration of mind. Some will decide to begin again as rays of Light to seed new worlds. Others hold the Cosmic Codes of Awakening. They will choose to continue their missions as Emissaries of The Light to help elevate and restore other worlds and future generations.

For most, life will progress according to the natural timeline. No longer hijacked or imprisoned by the Time Bandits of

Cosmic Consciousness or the rule of the Dark Order, they will unify within the crystalline consciousness of New Earth.

Love, peace, unity, truth, transparency, freedom, beauty, harmony, progress, and equality will radiate from The Light, bringing nourishment for humanity to regain their rightful heritage within the realm of Unified Conscious Creation. The qualities of Higher Consciousness will permeate New Earth with virtuous melodies that soothe old wounds and serenade the soul.

All is well, as the timeline is restored. A unified humanity holds the keys to unlocking the doors to the destiny of their greatest dreams and divine inheritance when they choose Love over fear and Truth over illusion.

30

DIVINITY SPEAKS

*T*he following transmission concludes the channeled messages in this book. It was received as the 2020 Pandemic was in its infancy, sweeping our world with confusion, fear, and disbelief.

Like the others, this message is not meant for me alone. It is for anyone who needs a reminder of the power of our thoughts, feelings, beliefs, words, and focus. These elements help us remember our truth, elevate our awareness, and break free from the illusions of a fear-based reality.

The more we unite as one human race, look beyond the programs of fear and conditioning, and trust our inner wisdom and higher knowing, the closer we come to rising to the New Earth that patiently waits for us to awaken and remember.

Transmission received from Divine Consciousness, March, 2020

Bring the Light Within to your awareness. Breathe, and feel the shift of peace and possibilities from the winds of higher transformation. Open the portals of your Enlightened Awareness as the world radiates a brighter tomorrow. Allow yourself to flow within the harmony of love, peace, and unity. Disengage from the imprisonment of fear, and the darkness of illusion.

The more you disconnect from a fear-based reality, and from what you are told to believe, your true self will shine. Your inner radiance will become evident not only to you, but to others. You will begin to remember the truth of who you are, as beings of Light and Love, within the holiness of the Divine One.

The shadow forces cannot prevail in the light of your truth. Your truth is within Me. It is within all things. I AM hope. I AM salvation. I AM Divinity within. Speak that into your day. Know this as who you are. All it takes is for you to remember. Awaken from the long dream of forgetfulness. Awaken to what is real—what has been hiding in plain sight.

Within you is the key to unlocking the door to higher realms, and deeper truth. Ask and it will be seen. Believe and it will be known. Lay down your differences in culture, politics, religion, race, and beliefs. We are all One in the Light of Divinity.

Together We unite in consciousness, thoughts, prayers, and meditation. Together We thrive in a seemingly broken world.

Together We illuminate the darkness for ourselves and others. Together We heal the world.

Turn inward for messages of hope, inspiration, and guidance. Divinity speaks to you within the silence of an open, loving heart, and a peaceful mind. Hold this message within you as your remembrance unfolds within the never-ending story of Life and Creation.

As you begin to awaken to the truth of your Divine Self, what has been hidden will become known. Those who see beyond the illusions will light the way for others, as they awaken to the truth of Reality.

From the dust of toppled illusions, control and fear-based agendas, a New Earth Rises. One that remembers its foundation of truth and transparency. One that is illuminated with Divine Light, and honors all forms of life and reality. A New Earth in which unconditional love, freedom, unity, peace, righteousness, justice, and harmony are tenants of the Radiance, and illuminate outcomes of the Word.

You have a choice to remain asleep in the dream of forgetfulness, or awaken to the long-lost dream of remembrance. Know that your Light Within is Divine Illumination. Trust in the glory and power of your Inner Radiance as a beacon for The Great Remembrance, and collective liberation of humanity—and say it is so.

AFTERWORD

Dear Awakened Dreamer,

Knowing the truth is not difficult. However, it can be uncomfortable to have your long-held beliefs shattered. It can be shocking to realize that the reality you have been taught and told to believe is merely a projection of our programming. This revelation may cause friendships to sever, families to separate, and livelihoods to crumble. While recognizing the truth is the easy part, seeing it and accepting it through the veil of lies and illusion is where the real work begins.

Many will deny the truth because they don't want to see it. They prefer to remain comfortably numb and righteously justified, obediently corralled within the familiarity of fear and the belief in limitation.

Standing in your truth is hard work when so many prefer to retreat into the blind dependency of the stories we are told. These narratives are strategically placed to keep us fighting among ourselves and perpetuate endless wars fueled by fear. I understand how the feelings of judgment and isolation can be lonely and suffocating as you struggle for the next breath of fresh reality.

Many with a mission to radiate The Light are awakening. The dream of forgetfulness is fading as we become more aware and draw strength from our remembrance of Divine Love and Unity Consciousness. As our eyes adjust to the brilliance of The Light, emerging from the darkness of fear and illusion, we begin to see with renewed clarity. The false narratives that once hypnotized us can no longer keep us imprisoned, separated, weak, or ignorant.

The thunder of our awakening rings the bells of The Great Liberation. The Great Remembrance serves as the bridge from the enslavement of our consciousness to the salvation of our society. Remember this if you need some strength:

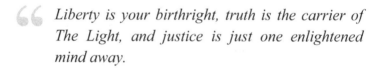 *Liberty is your birthright, truth is the carrier of The Light, and justice is just one enlightened mind away.*

My hope is for you to stay true to your mission. Remember, you are not alone. You are divinely guided, supported, and most importantly, loved. **Your spiritual awakening matters!** Every thought, action, feeling, emotion, deed, and word either contributes to The Great Awakening or keeps you blind and bound to the darkness. Choose powerfully and let your light shine brightly!

Each of us has a choice to make every second of our day. Please don't judge yourself if you stumble and fall into the hopeless pit of doubt, fear, and confusion. Reach out to each other for love and support. Reach inward for strength, insight, and courage.

Each moment is a new opportunity to rise up and choose again with renewed resolve, to win this war of all wars—the War on Consciousness. You do not need to be a slave to fear, or imprisoned within its order of darkness and deceit. There is Light to be remembered, and Ascension to be enjoyed.

You hold an essential page in the never-ending story of Life and Creation. Listen for the voice of Divinity to guide you and let love lead the way. Turn your attention away from the fear and programs that try to enslave you. Imagine and feel a brighter, happier, and better tomorrow with the depths of your heart and the song of your soul. The breath of Life and the birth of Creation are eternally inscribed within the divine flow of All That Is.

If you need a reminder on your journey return to this:

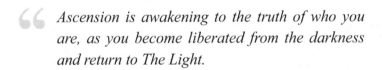

> *Ascension is awakening to the truth of who you are, as you become liberated from the darkness and return to The Light.*

You CAN do this. We WILL do this. In fact, it IS already done. Our tomorrow is created by the remembrance of our truth today. Right here and right now. Stand tall and be strong in your knowingness. Remember, you *are* The Light, you *are* Love, and you *are* The Way.

I know it's not easy, and you may feel tired, defeated, and alone, but you are not. We stand together, our love and energy reaching beyond the darkness, united in The Light.

Remember, free will and conscious creation are your birthright, empowering you to rise above the programs of conditioning and shape your destiny. By looking beyond the programs and aligning your intentions with the highest good, you become a beacon of light, guiding others toward a brighter future.

As we stand on the threshold of this new era, let us support each other with compassion and understanding. Though darkness has challenged us, it has revealed our strength and resilience. Now, we rise as one, ready to embrace the dawn of a new era.

Rest assured that the War on Consciousness will soon be a distant memory as we ascend to a unified, harmonious, and liberated New Earth.

All my love and blessings to you, dear Awakened One. Thank you for being the loving presence and heartful warrior who elevates the Earth Realm to its rightful inheritance, restoring our timeline to its natural order.

Shannon

ABOUT THE AUTHOR

Shannon MacDonald is a bestselling author, spiritual channel, and ascension guide known for her unique approach to navigating the complexities of spiritual awakening. Through soul-level guidance, intuitive insights, and energetic activations, she empowers individuals to expand their consciousness, transcend limiting beliefs, unlock dormant potentials, align with their higher purpose, and become conscious creators of their reality. Her books, services, and events serve as catalysts for spiritual alchemy, facilitating profound transformation, higher healing, and personal evolution.

Early in her 28-year career as a registered nurse, Shannon discovered her true calling as a healer, often witnessing profound and unexpected healing through energy work. This revelation ignited a lifelong quest to explore the deeper nature of energy and consciousness. She immersed herself in studying and integrating various energy healing modalities into both her personal and professional life. Through this journey, Shannon developed a deep awareness of the transformative power of energy and higher consciousness, which now guides her life's work.

Residing in Florida with her husband and their two dogs, Shannon finds joy in spending time with loved ones, connecting with nature, cycling, and riding motorcycles with her husband. As an Emissary of the Light, she is devoted to elevating the consciousness of humanity and the earthly realm, guiding those who seek a more purposeful and enlightened existence rooted in the love, light, unity, and truth of Divine Consciousness.

Shannon offers **Ascension Code Activations** and **Conscious Life Coaching**—transformative gateways designed to help individuals step into their true power and embody their soul's purpose. She also hosts **free Quantum Healing Events** and other life-changing experiences that support spiritual growth, enlightened living, and personal transformation. To learn more, explore her books, discover upcoming events, and schedule services, visit her website.

Visit Shannon's website to learn about her paradigm-shifting books, services, and events.
www.ShannonMacDonald.net

CONNECT WITH SHANNON

Follow Me on **YouTube** for inspirational messages, guided meditations and topics on awakening and ascension.
youtube.com/@ShannonMacdonaldAuthor

Follow me on **TikTok** for an authentic, unfiltered glimpse into my world.
tiktok.com/@shannonmacdonaldauthor

Sign up for my **mailing list** and receive advanced information about my upcoming books, events, and other news.
ShannonMacDonald.net/sign-up

BOOK REVIEW

HELP OTHER PEOPLE FIND MY BOOKS

If *New Earth Rising* brought value to your life, I would be deeply grateful if you could leave a review on Amazon and/or Goodreads.

As a self-published author, I don't have a marketing team—I have something even better: *YOU!* Your support, feedback, and shared experiences mean the world to me. Together, we can inspire others to discover this work and awaken to their higher purpose and true potentials.

Thank you for being part of this journey!

Shannon MacDonald

ALSO BY SHANNON MACDONALD

Navigating Ascension Symptoms
A Guide to Spiritual Awakening and Higher Healing

Free eBook!

This power-packed, quick-read book demystifies the ascension process and equips you with practical tools to navigate the cosmic rollercoaster of Ascension Symptoms with clarity and confidence.

Free Download on Shannon's website
or buy the print and ebook on Amazon

ShannonMacDonald.net/all-books

New Earth Reality
The Other Side of Ascension
The Great Liberation

Coming Soon

Sequel to New Earth Rising

As humanity nears The Great Liberation and Ascension to the New Earth, *The Other Side of Ascension* explores crucial questions and new insights about human consciousness and the next phase of Reality.

ShannonMacDonald.net/all-books

Mastering Manifestation
12 Keys to Unlock Your Hidden Potential and Live the Life of Your Dreams

The awakened seeker's guide to practical alchemy and Conscious Creation.

Unlock the 12 Keys to transform your life from within, magnetize success, and supercharge your magnetic qualities to thrive in all areas—regardless of the world around you.

ShannonMacDonald.net/all-books

Made in the USA
Las Vegas, NV
18 April 2025

21077887R10089